Praise for HOT ROD Activity Books

"This is the most comprehensive set of literacy activities I have seen in one book!" **- Dannah Fritz Co-Owner of Jacksonville Tutoring Specialists, Advanced Certified in Barton & Accredited IEW Instructor**

"As an SLP, I highly recommend Dean's HOT ROD Activity Books to my colleagues! I love these books because they simultaneously target articulation, oral language, and literacy skills. It's a comprehensive tool that not only improves speech but also supports overall language development! This is a must-have for any SLP!" **- Ellen Cieszkiewicz Rigg, M.A. CCC-SLP, A/OGA**

What a powerful tool for anyone supporting learners! The Comprehension section includes practical strategies to assist learners as they explore texts. Students' comprehension will be supported by using the PAGES framework to help them think critically about the text they're reading. This chapter also gives learners signal words and practice paragraphs to help determine what type of text they're reading. Dean's story "Bats and Their Amazing Skills" is followed by comprehension questions and the opportunity to cite and explain an answer using the RACE framework. Students' skills and confidence will grow if they utilize these strategies." **-Jolene Gutierrez, M.L.S., author of *Too Much! An Overwhelming Day*, teacher/librarian at Denver Academy, a school for neurodivergent learners including those with dyslexia**

Gods and Gifts
Activity Book
by
Carolee Dean, MS, CCC-SLP, CALT

based on

Gods and Gifts:

Three Greek Myths Retold

(No Gift for Man, The Bandit, & The Box)

by Carolee Dean

Word Travel Press LLC - Littleton, CO

HOT ROD – Higher **O**rder **T**hinking
through the **R**eading **o**f **D**ecodables

Gods and Gifts
Activity Book
by Carolee Dean

based on
Gods and Gifts:
Three Greek Myths Retold
A HOT ROD Decodable Book
Level 1
Closed Syllables (Short Vowels)
Consonant Blends
Suffix -s, -ness, less, ful

Find the Scope & Sequence for the Series at
www.wordtravelpress.com
Word Travel Press LLC - Littleton, CO

Contents

INTRODUCTORY MATERIAL

About the Author.. 9

Additional Resources... 10

Target Users.. 12

Tips for Speech-Language Pathologists.. 13

Pair and Share Reading... 14

How to Use This Resource... 15

Reading Levels & Supports by Grade Level... 16

Copy and Memorize Strategy... 17

Fluency and Accuracy... 18

Components of Reading Overview... 19

Written Language Overview.. 20

Online Use... 21

ACTIVITY SECTIONS

Decoding, Articulation, and Spelling... 22

Target Words... 23

Multi-Syllable Words... 25

/s/ words.. 26

/r/ words.. 28

Learned Words.. 29

Names & Places... 30

Card Game Instructions... 31

Game Card Template... 32

Word Cards... 33

Four-In-Row Game Boards.. 66

Word and Sentence Dictation.. 79

Contents

Phonological Awareness (including trochaic tetrameter).............................. 83

    Say It Again, Sam: Sound and Syllable Deletion........................... 85

    Sound Tracks: Tracking Sound Changes.................................. 90

    Feel the Beat: Prosody and Rhythm..................................... 92

    Rhyme Time #1-2: Rhyme and Alliteration................................ 96

    Rhyme Time #3-4: Finish the Poem..................................... 100

    Rhyme Time #5: Write Your Own.. 103

Cognitive Flexibility.. 104

    Category Sorts: Animals & Actions...................................... 107

    Category Sorts: Final /s/ and /z/...................................... 108

    Multiple Classification Task... 109

Morphology.. 111

    Morpho Mania #1 Compound Words... 115

    Morpho Mania #2-3 Suffix *-s*... 117

    Morpho Mania #4 Suffix *-ful, -ness, -less*........................... 121

    Morpho Mania #5 Suffix -en.. 123

    Morpho Mania #6 Prefix **pro**.. 125

    Morpho Mania #7 Word Sums for **rest**................................ 127

    Morpho Mania #8 Word Sums for **help**................................ 129

    Morpho Mania #9 Word Sums for **spect**............................... 131

    Morpho Mania #10 Etymology of Names................................... 134

Vocabulary.. 135

    Word Clues – Seek and Find.. 137

    Multiple Meaning Match Up #1-3.. 139

    WOW Vocabulary Terms #1 *No Gift for Man*............................. 142

    WOW Vocabulary Terms #2 – 5 *The Bandit*.............................. 143

    WOW Vocabulary Terms #6 – The Box..................................... 147

    WOW Vocabulary Terms #7 – "Bats and Their Amazing Skills"... 148

    WOW Vocabulary Terms #8 – Background Information.............. 149

    Vocabulary Foldable... 151

Contents

Sentence Construction.. 153

    Sentence Mania: Verb, Noun, or Adjective........................... 154

    Sentence Construction #1-2: Coordinating Conjunctions......... 156

    Sentence Construction #3: Who is Doing What?...................... 160

    Sentence Construction#4: Identifying Complete Sentences..... 161

Story Frames – Plot Analysis... 163

Comprehension.. 167

    PAGES Strategy...
168

    Text Type Guide.. 169

    What's My Text Type.. 170

    Non-Fiction Connection: "Bats and Their Amazing Skills"..... 173

    Comprehension Questions – Bats.............................. 177

    RACE Responses - Bats... 179

    Comprehension Questions – *The Bandit*.................. 180

    RACE Responses – *The Bandit*.............................. 182

Graphic Organizers for Paragraph & Essay Writing............................. 183

    What's Your Gift?... 184

    Fun Facts List.. 185

    Before & After Balloon Brainstorm........................... 186

    Greek & Maya Cultures – Balloon Brainstorm.................. 187

    Venn Diagram – Epimetheus and Prometheus.................... 188

    Venn Diagram – Bats and Birds................................ 189

    High Five Paragraph Writing.................................... 190

    IPPC Compare & Contrast Essay............................ 193

Contents

Create.. 197

    Animal Fun Facts.. 198

    The Uses of Fire.. 199

    Animal Gifts and Habitats.................................. 200

    Funny Hobbies for Zeus..................................... 201

    Writing with WOW Words..................................... 203

    Pandora's Lunch Box.. 204

    Create a Myth.. 207

HOT Topics.. 208

References.. 212

HOT ROD Titles.. 214

About the Author

Direct questions or comments to:
info@wordtravelpress.com

Carolee Dean, MS, CCC-SLP, CALT is a board-certified speech-language pathologist and a dyslexia interventionist with 20 years of experience working in public schools. She is a former president of the Southwest Branch of the International Dyslexia Association, a Regional Representative for IDA, and a frequent speaker at educational conferences. Dean serves as an adjunct instructor in the Master's in Literacy and Special Education program at Providence College and is the author of *Story Frames for Teaching Literacy: Enhancing Student Learning Through the Power of Storytelling* (Paul H. Brookes Publishing Co., 2021).

Dean is also a children's author of award-winning young adult titles: *Comfort* (Houghton Mifflin), *Take Me There* (Simon Pulse: A Division and Simon and Schuster), a YALSA Quick Pick for Reluctant Readers, and *Forget Me Not* (Simon Pulse), a novel in verse

Dean has combined her love of children's literature and her passion for helping struggling readers to create the HOT ROD Series – **H**igher **O**rder **T**hinking through the **R**eading **o**f **D**ecodables. The purpose of the series is to provide older struggling readers with meaningful text that connects to the curriculum. Because of her background in language development and speech-language pathology, each book is accompanied by activities to foster growth in all the components of reading as well as language development and articulation. For additional resources see the information on the next page.

HOT ROD - Higher Order Thinking
through the Reading Of Decodables

Additional Resources

The chapter book, *Gods and Gifts: Three Greek Myths Retold* is a decodable chapter book illustrated in black and white for older students (grades 4-8 and above). It contains the same stories as the three decodable, full-color, illustrated picture books, *No Gift for Man, The Bandit, and The Box* for younger students (grades 3-4). The chapter book also includes extensive background information on ancient writing systems and a comparison to indigenous creation stories.

All four books may be found online at Amazon, Barnes & Noble, or your favorite local bookstore. Simply go to your bookstore's website. When you get to the SEARCH option, type in the title of the book. Another option is to visit Bookshop.org. Find a variety of purchasing options at www.wordtravelpress.com.

Schools and Libraries may purchase books from Ingram in paperback, hardcover, and e-book formats. An audiobook of *Gods and Gifts* is available for the chapter book - story, and background information only.

For information about bulk orders and purchase orders, contact info@wordtravelpress.com.

You will need either the chapter book or the three picture books to get the full benefit of the material in this activity guide. The engaging illustrations provide students with the experience of reading a real book. They may be sent home for fluency practice. Students may enjoy owning their own copy to read again and again. If sending the book home, be sure to include a copy of the page that explains the Pair and Share Reading Strategy.

See additional supplementary activities on the next page.

Decodable Chapter Book & Audio Book

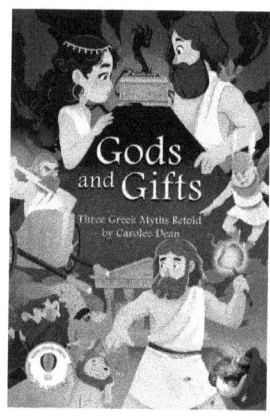

Decodable Picture Books

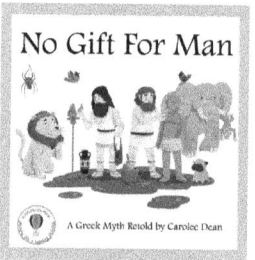

Additional Resources

Four in a Row Games: 10 Virtual Board Games provide fun practice for closed syllables, /s/ blends, and /r/ blends using the Target Words found in the poem stories in *Gods and Gifts*. It is available for a small additional fee. Go to https://wow.boomlearning.com and explore **Store>Word Travel Press.** Additional FREE digital resources are available on that page including the Cognitive Flexibility activity focusing on final /s/ and /z/.

FREE RESOURCES

Additional FREE resources below are for Level 1 of the HOT ROD Series (*Gods and Gifts* which includes the poems from *No gift for Man, The Bandit*, and *The Box.* They are provided at no charge as an introduction to the supplemental resources found in the HOT ROD series.

Story Plot Analysis – *The Creation of Man* Story Analysis incorporates the books mentioned above. It is available as a free download at http://www.wordtravelpress.com on the tab for COR Instruction on the Resources page.

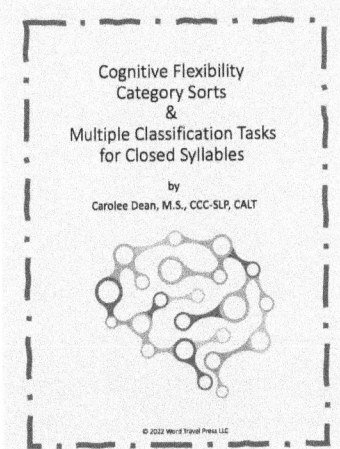

Cognitive Flexibility - The *Cognitive Flexibility Category Sorts & Multiple Classification Tasks for Closed Syllables* is a 38-page PDF filled with lists containing closed syllable words that can be cut out and sorted according to a variety of categories. The printable paper version is free. A digital version is available on Boom Cards for a small fee. Go to the website and under the Resources tab, look for Cognitive Flexibility.

Find additional books and resources as well as the scope and sequence for the HOT ROD series, at https://www.wordtravelpress.com. Sign up for the newsletter on the webpage to keep up with book news, articles of interest, and free offers.

Target Users

The chapter book, *Gods and Gifts: Three Greek Myths Retold,* and the picture books, *No Gift for Man, The Bandit,* and *The Box,* align with Level 1 of the HOT ROD Series- Higher Order Thinking through the Reading of Decodables. It was written primarily for students in grades 4 and up who still need work on decoding words that contain closed (short) vowels and consonant blends. The story is appropriate for use with general education students as well.

This Activity Book includes word lists along with numerous activities that focus on the Components of Reading (COR) that support reading comprehension and writing. Go to www.wordtravelpress.com to find the Scope and Sequence of the series.

Students with a sixth-grade reading level or higher may read the entire book including the introduction independently. Younger students and struggling readers may listen to the introduction read aloud and read the story poem themselves with support.

Books from the HOT ROD Series can be used to supplement any reading program but were specifically designed to support Orton-Gillingham based instruction. Level 1 may contain more elements than are traditionally taught to beginning readers. That is because these stories and poems were designed as a review and consolidation of concepts. They are also intended for older readers who often have a higher sight word vocabulary than younger readers as well as more exposure to suffixes and prefixes. The story may be used at any point after all closed syllable (short vowel) sounds from Level 1 and single consonants in blends have been introduced. Students should also be familiar with the concept of suffix s (sounding as both /s/ and /z/). Students should be introduced to the idea that the unstressed vowel in a multi-syllable words may sound like a schwa ("uh"). The chapter book and the activities in this guide were designed to reinforce the concepts outlined above.

Speech-Language Pathologists
16 Ways to Address Articulation of /r/ and /s/ using *Gods and Gifts*

An SLP can use the material in the **Gods and Gifts Activity Book** to work on goals in all the areas listed in the Components of Reading Overview. Many of the skills that make a student a good reader also promote strong oral language skills. However, since many SLPs focus on articulation and speech sound production, the activities listed below help to illustrate how students can work on the /s/ and /r/ sounds in a variety of contexts. In this way, SLPs can support numerous reading skills while working on speech goals.

Word Level
Card Games may be played with the one and two-syllable words on the flashcards (pp.33-65)

Four-in-a-Row Gameboards (p. 77-78) focus on /s/ in a variety of positions as well as /r/ blends in initial position.

Phonological Awareness incorporates initial sound deletion in /s/ blends on p. 87 and medial /s/ deletion on p. 89.

Sound Tracks on p. 90 students move one letter tile at a time to create new words as spoken by the therapist. They must make the sound change where they hear the change. List 1 starts with Initial /s/ blends while List 2 focuses on Final /s/ blends. A Free Boom Card activity allows students to move digital letters.

Sentence Level
Dictation activities on (pp. 79-82) may be used to read sentences with target /s/ and /r/ blends.

Cognitive Flexibility (p. 104-110) Sort 12 words into these categories: Final /s/ vs. Final /z/ and Animals vs. Actions. Then complete a multi-classification grid requiring that the student consider all categories at the same time.

Morpho Mania #2 (pp. 117-118) explores sentences with words that end in suffix –s.

Morpho Mania #6 (p. 125) explores words and sentences using the Latin Prefix PRO.

Morpho Mania #7 (p. 127), students use a word matrix to create word sums using the base element *rest* and suffixes *-ness, -less*. Then they use the word sums to complete sentences.

Morpho Mania #9 (p. 131) does the same thing with the base element *spect*.

Word Clues: Seek and Find (p. 137) incorporates /s/ words in an activity that helps students improve their ability to use context to determine word meaning.

Sentence Mania: Noun, Verb, Adjective (p. 154) requires students to determine if underlined words are functioning as a verb, noun, or an adjective within a sentence. Sentences contain several /s/ words.

Paragraph Level & Extended Text
What's My Text Type (pp.169-171) Students read paragraphs and use signal words to decide on the text type being used (ie. description, sequence, compare/contrast, problem/solution, etc).

Gods and Gifts chapter book (sold separately). Students read the story poems incorporating numerous /s/ and /r/ words as they read aloud.

Pandora's Lunch Box (pp. 204-206). Make a list of disgusting /r/ and /s/ foods, use them in a poem, and read it aloud.

Discourse Level
Story Frames Plot Analysis (p.163). Students retell the story from *Gods and Gifts* using the Plot Analysis storyboard as a guide.

Pair and Share Reading

Pair and Share Reading is a strategy incorporated in the HOT ROD series that *pairs* developing readers with proficient readers (educators, parents, peers) who *share* the literacy experience by reading the more challenging segments of a text aloud while the developing reader reads the portions that are targeted for their decoding level.

The reading partner may be a reading interventionist, speech-language pathologist, or other educator working 1:1 or in a small group with students. In the classroom, teachers can more strategically assign portions of books to be read aloud by students at very different reading levels. Teachers may also pair struggling readers with more advanced ones to work together as reading partners. In the Background Section of the chapter book, each paragraph has been analyzed for grade level.

The stories from the HOT ROD series are perfect for parents who want to support the reading instruction happening at school or other settings. The books can be sent home for additional reading practice or parents may incorporate them on their own in consultation with a teacher, therapist, or reading tutor.

Finally, homeschoolers may use books from the series along with the Pair and Share strategy to provide reading fluency practice and to introduce their children to content at or beyond their current reading level. In fact, exposure to rich content is at the heart of the strategy. The activities may be used to work on a variety of skills across age and ability levels.

For information about the Scope and Sequence of the HOT ROD series and to find additional titles, go to https://wordtravelpress.com/.

Chapter books are also available as audiobooks. Check the website for details.

How to Use This Resource

Scope and Sequence - Look at the scope and sequence for Level 1 to make sure the story aligns with the student's current decoding skill level. If not, words that contain unfamiliar patterns should be pre-taught as learned words. Concepts such as schwa in unstressed syllables should be introduced prior to reading.

Practice Reading Target Words – Patterns targeted for Level 1 are short vowels (**a** – apple, **e** – elephant, **i** – igloo, **o** – octopus, **u** – umbrella). If students need additional practice with closed (short) vowels or consonant blends, they may read the Words-In-Sentences in the Dictation section for reading practice. Practice the Target Word Lists to make sure the student is accurate 90% of the time before they read the story poems.

Learned Words - Learned words must be taught prior to reading either because they contain an irregular pattern or because they include a pattern that has not yet been taught. If the student is not familiar with these words, practice them using the Copy & Memorize strategy described later in this Activity Book.

Pre-teach Vocabulary – Introduce unfamiliar vocabulary terms from the story before reading. Do the same for the vocabulary terms that go with the Background Information section.

Access Prior Knowledge – Before reading the story, share prior knowledge about fire through a class discussion. Have the class work together to make a list of the many uses of fire.

Work on Component Skills – Students often struggle with reading because of weakness in underlying skills other than or in addition to decoding. This resource is filled with supplementary materials to work on phonological awareness, cognitive flexibility, morphology, vocabulary, sentence structure, written language, and more. Pick and choose the activities that best support your students' current needs. See pages 19-20 for a description of each of the categories addressed in the Activity Book.

Data Collection – See specific directions for calculating fluency. For activity pages, simply divide the number of correct responses by the total number of possible responses for a % correct. An approximate grade level has been provided for each section. Boom Cards may also be used for data collection.

Collaboration – Classroom teachers, reading interventionists, and speech-language pathologists may easily collaborate to explore different activities based on the same story content. Each professional may use the activities that support their goals and objectives for a particular student or classroom.

Reading Levels & Supports by Grade Level

Grades 5+ - Students with grade 5 skills and above should be able to read much of the book independently. Encourage them to study the key terms and name pronunciations first. The information can then be used to work on written responses and higher-order thinking activities.

Grades 4- Students may read the entire book with instructional support after vocabulary terms and names are formally introduced. They may need help parsing longer sentences and phrases. Question them often and have conversations to check for understanding. Pause and picture what is happening in the story and ask clarifying questions.

Grade 3- Students may practice reading the Target Words and Learned Words aloud. If accuracy is above 90%, they may read the decodable story with support after listening to the Introduction section for each story poem. If accuracy is below 90%, they should continue practicing the target words and the sentences in the Dictation section until they can read them with ease, or they should listen to the story being read aloud. Introduce the concepts of visualizing and self-questioning. Pick and choose what Background Information sections to share based on what is age-appropriate and relevant to the curriculum.

Level 1 Decoding (Use with any grade)

Regardless of age or grade level, students working at decoding Level 1 of the HOT ROD Scope and Sequence (found at https://wordtravelpress.com) or a similar program should follow the steps below:

1. Practice reading the Target Words and Learned Words to 90% accuracy or higher.

2. Listen to an explanation of the Key Terms.

3. Listen to the Introduction read aloud. Pause and picture what is happening in the story. Practice self-questioning when information is confusing.

4. The student reads the Decodable Story Poem out loud to a reading partner.

6. Discuss the HOT TOPIC questions.

Copy and Memorize Strategy

Decodable books and stories use words based on syllable patterns that the student has been taught strategically and systematically, but they typically also contain some phonetically irregular words that cannot be decoded. These words only make up about 5-10% of the English language, but they occur frequently in books and in spoken language. Their use should be limited ideally to 5% of a text or less in decodable books. We call these words **Learned Words**, though other programs may use different terminology. They need to be pretaught before reading a decodable book using the steps below. In addition, if a text contains words that are regular but based on patterns that have not yet been introduced, they should be taught as learned words for the text to be considered decodable.

Say – Say the word out loud and have the student repeat it.

Copy – Have students copy the word from a model, naming each letter as they write it. End with saying the whole word out loud again. Start with near-point copying with the word next to where the student is writing. Evolve to far-point copying with the word on a whiteboard five or more feet away. They may also start with **tracing** the word that someone else has written and then make a copy next to it.

Check – Instruct the student to check to make sure they have copied the word correctly. If not, repeat steps one and two.

Study – Look at the parts of the word and determine what sounds are spelled in an unexpected way. Which sounds are regular for spelling?

Copy – Copy the word again. Start with saying the word out loud. Copy it naming each letter. Say the word again after it has been written.

Memorize – Cover the word and write it from memory. Tell students to name each letter as they write it and end by saying the whole word out loud again.

Check – Uncover the word and check for accuracy. If needed, repeat the steps.

Fluency and Accuracy

Repeated Readings – Reading a text multiple times has been shown to increase fluency speed and accuracy (National Reading Panel, 2000). Many of the stories in the HOT ROD Series incorporate poetry which naturally lends itself to repeated readings. In addition, because HOT ROD books involve engaging and high-quality content, students are excited to circle back to these selections as their decoding skills improve when they can read the entire book independently.

Calculating Accuracy and identifying Miscues for Decodable Passages - While the student reads aloud from the decodable poems, tally errors. You may calculate a percent correct, but poetry cannot be assessed for grade level because of unconventional punctuation use. Track student errors by using a counter clicker or tally on a piece of paper by making hash marks. If you want to record more detailed information about types of errors, use the following code: SC= self-corrections, I = insertions, R = repetitions, O = omissions, S = substitutions, and D = delays of more than 2 seconds.

Reading Fluency for Grade Level Passages – The introduction and background information portions are not decodable, but they have been analyzed according to ATOS to calculate an approximate grade level. You may derive fluency scores based on grade-level expectations from the introductory and background sections. Each reading passage is calculated separately so that measures of reading fluency may be assessed as desired. ATOS uses a readability formula based on average sentence length, average word length, and word difficulty level. To find out more about ATOS, visit https://www.renaissance.com/edword/atos/.

Calculate Accuracy –
Total Words Per Section – Errors = Total Correct.
Total Correct ÷ Total Words Per Section   = % Correct
Timed Reading Samples - You may want to time reading speed and calculate the number of words read accurately per minute, but please discontinue this practice if the student rushes, becomes anxious, or begins to use old, ineffective strategies like guessing.

Prosody – To work on prosody (patterns of stressed and unstressed syllables) see the activity called *Feel the Beat*.

Reference: Eunice Kennedy Shriver National Institute of Child Health and Human Development, NIH, DHHS. (2000). Report of the National Reading Panel: Teaching Children to Read: Reports of the Subgroups (00-4754). Washington, DC: U.S. Government Printing Office.

Components of Reading Overview

Note: The HOT Topics page at the end of this Activity Book explains how the activities listed below fit into the 24 categories of Bloom's Revised Taxonomy. The icons to the left are found on the activity pages that support that skill.

Decoding & Articulation Practice and Pre-reading:
Target Words – Read the columns of words as a preview before reading the story. Tally errors and calculate a baseline based on the number of words in each column. Totals appear in gray under the word lists. Retest after reading the story and completing the activities of your choice. Sentences are available for additional practice for one-syllable target words on the Boom Cards and in the dictation section of this book. For articulation cards, you may want to create cards for the Memory Game or Go Fish. **Learned Words** – Practice the Copy & Memorize Strategy.

Phonological Awareness:
Say It Again, Sam - Students work on deletion by repeating words and leaving out sounds or syllables.
Sound Tracks- Change one sound at a time to create new words.
Feel the Beat – Underline stressed words in the poem and practice reading with prosody and stress.
Rhyme Time – Circle rhymes, underline alliterations, and write a sentence containing an alliteration. Generate words to complete a poem following a pattern of stressed and unstressed syllables. Create lines of an original poem.

Cognitive Flexibility: The *Cognitive Flexibility Category Sorts & Multiple Classification Tasks for Closed Syllables* is a 38- page PDF filled with lists containing closed syllable words that can be sorted according to a variety of categories. It is available for Free on the website. Digital Boom Cards are also available online.

Morphology: **Morpho Mania:** Explore Suffix **–s**, is it plural, possessive, or action? Does it sound like /s/ or /z/? Explore the Prefix **PRO**. Suffix –**ful, --ness, -less, -en. Structured Word Inquiry**: Use a matrix to build word sums for base elements **rest, help, spect**. Use the word sums for sentences. **Etymology** – Prometheus, Epimetheus, Pandora

Vocabulary: Create **Vocabulary Foldables**. Play a Matching Game with multiple meaning words. Explore vocabulary using **Context Clues** by reading information from the background section of the chapter book and searching the surrounding sentences for clues to word meaning.

Written Language Overview

Sentence Awareness and Sentence Construction:

Sentence Mania – Decide if underlined words are acting like nouns, verbs, or adjectives.

Sentence Combining - Combine short sentences into longer ones using the coordinating conjunctions provided.

Who is Doing What? – Answer WH- questions to build sentences.

Plot Structure, Story Retells, & Summaries:

Story Plot Analysis – *The Creation of Man* Story Analysis incorporates the three myths highlighted in the chapter book, *Gods and Gifts*. They come from the first three books of the HOT ROD series: *No Gift for Man*, *The Bandit,* and *The Box*.

Comprehension:

PAGES – This strategy includes Picturing, Asking, Going Back (or Forward) Exploring, and Summarizing. **What's My Test Type?:** Use the Signal Words in the Text Type Guide to determine the text type being used in six different paragraphs. **Comprehension Questions** - Read the Non-Fiction piece on "Bats and Their Amazing Skills." Answer the open-ended questions either verbally or in writing. Practice answering in complete sentences by restating the question before providing an answer.

RACE Responses – Follow the directions to turn the short answers into complete RACE responses to Restate, Answer, Cite, and Explain.

Notetaking & Graphic Organizers:

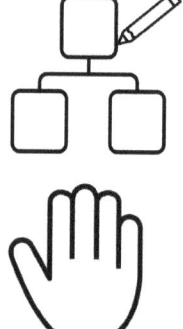

Graphic Organizers for Paragraph & Essay Writing:

Fun Facts - Brainstorm a list to explore what life was like before and after the discovery of fire. **Venn Diagrams and Balloon Brainstorms –** Use two different formats to compare and contrast a variety of topics.

High Five Writing – Use the High Five template to brainstorm paragraphs based on writing prompts. **Compare/Contrast Essay** - Use the I+P+P+C directions to construct a multi-paragraph Compare & Contrast essay.

Create:

The highest level of Bloom's Taxonomy involves synthesizing what has been learned to create something new. This section contains a variety of fun and engaging creative writing prompts, including **Funny Hobbies for Zeus** and **Pandora's Lunch Box.**

HOT Topics – Explore this section to learn how the activities described above fit into the 24 categories of Bloom's Revised Taxonomy.

Online Use

1. For online learning, mail the chapter book, *Gods and Gifts: Three Greek Myths Retold* to the student OR use the e-book version of the chapter book and share it using Screen Share. Permission is granted for tele-education purposes. Email Activity Book pages to the school or home or upload pages onto Google Classroom. Activity pages may be printed wherever the student is located.

2. Boom Cards may be used to play online games. Some Boom Cards are free, and some require an additional fee.

3. Check all links to any online resources such as Boom Cards to make sure they are still accessible and appropriate. Some sites such as YouTube contain ads and should be avoided or closely monitored depending on the setting.

4. You may display your PDFs for students using the SCREEN SHARE feature of Zoom. You may also display any pages of the Activity Book using a document camera. A cell phone may be used in place of a document camera. You may turn on the ANNOTATE feature of Zoom to type or write on the PDF to show students examples of how to construct written responses or add diacritical coding marks to words.It will not save as you scroll, but you may take a screenshot if desired. If you have Adobe Pro, students may type directly on the PDF in edit mode.

5. Via the SCREEN SHARE feature of Zoom, give students the ability to share their screen with you so you can see their written computer work. If they are using pencil and paper, they may hold up their work or use a document camera to share it. They may also complete work in Google Classroom.

6. Online games may be shared using SCREEN SHARE. Use caution if you give students REMOTE CONTROL access since they are basically taking over your screen. Some educators prefer the option of having students give them verbal directions while playing games. Never display your entire desktop using Screen Share.

7. Note that if the student is using a Chrome Book, the Remote-Control feature will likely not be available on Zoom.

DECODING & ARTICULATION

INTRODUCTION

Articulation - Speech-language pathologists using this resource to work on speech-sound production of /s/, /z/ and /r/ have many options. See page 23 for the 15 Different Ways to Address Articulation. Words are listed by sound groups in this section, but flashcard word cards are not grouped according to the /s/, /z/, and /r/ sounds. You will need to pull those from the other lists. They are separated on the Boom Cards.

DECODING:

Target Words - Have students practice reading words BEFORE and AFTER reading the story. Compare performance. Use the word lists that follow and/or flashcards for decoding practice. Make two sets of cards to play Go Fish or the Memory Game. Sentences in the Dictation section may be used for reading practice at the sentence level.

Learned Words – Have students practice these using the Copy and Memory Strategy.

Four-in-a-Row – Students use a fun game format to practice finding words that contain closed vowels in a variety of contexts (CVC, CCVC, CVCC, CCVCC, /s/, and /r/). This game is available on Boom Cards for an additional fee.

Online resources, including free flash cards, may be found at https://wow.boomlearning.com. Explore Store>Word Travel Press.

Calculate Accuracy: While the student reads each target word aloud, tally errors. The number of words per column appears below that column. Subtract 1 point if they make an error and don't self-correct. Subtract half a point for self-corrections, repetitions, or delays of more than 2 seconds. Add up Errors. Subtract this total from the total number of words per column. This is the Total Number Correct. Divide the Total Number Correct by the Total Number Per Column = % correct.

Target Words
One-Syllable (a and e)
from *Gods and Gifts*
by Carolee Dean

Word List #1– Practice these words either by reading the lists below or using the flashcards on the following pages. Some words are also available for free on Boom Cards. The words with an asterisk * should be first introduced as LEARNED WORDS

Patterns	Words	Total
One Syllable		
ă	an, and, ant, as, asp, at, bad, band, bass, bat, blast, brass, camp, can, cat, class, crab, craft, crag, cramp, drag, fast, gal grab, grand, had, ham, jam, lamp, land, lass, last, man, nab, nap, pad, pan, pant, pass, past, plan, plant, ran, rant, rat, sag, sand, scab, scads, scalp, scam, scan, slam, spat, strand, swam, *that, trap, vast, wax	/60
ĕ	bell, bend, best, crept, crest, den, dress, egg, fed, fell, fled, get, glen, help, kept, leg, left, let, melt, men, mess, met, nest, pelt, pest, red, rend, rest, send, sent, set, *shell, slept, smell, smelt, sped, stem, strep, stress, swept, tell, *them, *then, web, wed, well, went *when, yen	/49

Target Words
One-Syllable (i, o, u)
from *Gods and Gifts*
by Carolee Dean

Word List #1 (continued)– Practice these words either by reading the lists below or using the flashcards on the following pages. Some words are also available for free on Boom Cards. The words with an asterisk * should be first introduced as LEARNED WORDS

Patterns	Words	Total
One Syllable		
ĭ	bit, bliss, cliff, did, dim, drift, drill, fill, fin, fist, fit, flip, frill, gift, glint, grin, grit, hid, hill, him, hint, hip, hiss, in, it, is, lid, lift, limp, lip, lit, milk, mint, mumps, nip, pig, pit, rip, silk, sit, skill, slip, spill, spin, spit, split, swift, tin, trip, twig, twist, will, wilt, wind, *with	/55
ŏ	bog, bond, box, dog, drop, flop, fox, frog, gloss, god, got, hog, hop, hot, log, loss, moss, not, on, pond, pox, rot, slop, sod, spot, stop, top, toss, trod, trot	/30
ŭ	bluff, bump, but, cut, dusk, dust, grunt, hunt, just, lump, mud, pug, puss, rust, slug, slum, stuff, trust, up	/19

Multi-Syllable Words

from *Gods and Gifts*
by Carolee Dean

Word List #2–Practice these words either by reading the lists below or using the flashcards on the following pages . The words with an asterisk * should be first introduced as LEARNED WORDS

Patterns	Words	Total
Two-syllable	a·**bet,** an·vil, at·tic, ban·dit, bas·set, bliss·ful, bob·cat, bot·tom, can·non, can·yon, com·bat, com·mon, con·flict, con·stant, con·tents, con·vict, crim·son, den·tist, dis·mal, dis·tant, dras·tic, en·**trust,** fal·con, fen·nel, fran·tic, fret·ful, fun·nel, gal·lant, grand·est, help·ful, hid·den, hun·dred, hus·band, ill·ness, in·sult, jac·kal, kin·dred, land·fills, lin·net, mat·tress, pros·pect, pub·lic, pum·mel, rab·bit, ras·cal, rot·ten, rus·tic, scan·dal, sil·ken, sis·kin, sod·den, splen·did, sud·den, sul·len, sum·mit, tem·pest, traf·fic, trod·den, tun·nel, van·dal, ven·om, ves·pid, Vul·can, wist·ful, *with·in, wit·less	/66
Three-Syllable	dis·con·**tent**·ment, fan·**tas**·tic, *for·**bid**·den, in·**dig**·nant, prob·lem·**at**·tic, rap·id·ness	/6
Stress on later syllable	a·**bet,** dis·con·**tent**·ment, en·**trust,** fan·**tas**·tic, *for·**bid**·den, in·**dig**·nant, prob·lem·**at**·tic	/7

S Words
from *Gods and Gifts*
by Carolee Dean

Word List #3–Practice these words either by reading the lists below or using the flashcards on the following pages. These lists feature /s/ next to a consonant sometimes in a blend, sometimes as a suffix, and sometimes in separate syllables. The words with an asterisk * should be first introduced as LEARNED WORDS. Many of these words are also available for free as Boom Cards at https://wow.boomlearning.com. Explore Store>Word Travel Press.

Patterns	Words	Total
Initial s	sag, sand, send, set, sit, so	**/6**
Final s	bliss, brass, class, dress, gloss, hiss, lass, loss, mess, moss, pass, puss, stress, toss	**/14**
Initial Blends	scab, scads, scalp, scan, scum, skill, slam, slept, slip, slop, smell, smelt, spat, sped, spill, spin, spit, split, spot, stem, stop, strand, strep, stress, stuff, swam, swept, swift	**/28**
Final Blends	asp, best, blast, box, crest, dusk, dust, fast, fox, just, last, nest, past, pest, pox, rest, rust, test, trust, twist, vast, wax	**/22**
Suffix -s = /s/	ants, bits, bumps, camps, cats, drifts, fists, fits, hints, hips, glints, lamps, limps, lips, lumps, mumps, nests, pants, pests, pits, plants, rats, spits, traps, twists	**/25**

S Multi-Syllable Words

from *Gods and Gifts*
by Carolee Dean

Word List #4–See the instructions on the previous page.

Patterns	Words	Total
Initial	sil·ken, sud·den, sum·mit (blends) scan ·dal, splen·did	/5
Medial	bliss·ful, con·stant, den·tist, dis·tant, dras·tic, en·**trust**, fan·**tas**·tic, grand·est, in·sult, pros·pect, ras·cal, rus·tic sis·kin, tem·pest, ves·pid, wist·ful	/16
Final	end·less, ill·ness, mat·tress, wit·less	/4
Suffix -s = /s/	ban·dits, con·tents, con·victs, in·sults	/4

/z/ Words

Patterns	Words	Total
Suffix –s =/z/	bands, bells, bogs, bonds, bugs, bums, dens, dogs, drills, eggs, frills, glens, gods, grins, hills, hogs, jams, lands, legs, logs, man's, pads, pans, plans, ponds, scads, skills, slams, slugs, slums, spills, stems, strands, twigs, webs, weds	/36
/z/ Multi-syllable	(suffix –s) can·nons, land·fills, ras·cals, scan·dals, van·dals (non-suffix) crim·son, dis·mal, hus·band	/8

R Words

from *Gods and Gifts*
by Carolee Dean

Word List #5–See the instructions on the previous page.

Patterns	Words	Total
Initial R	ran, rant, rat, red, rend, rest, rip, rot, rust	/9
Multi-Syllable	rab·bit, rap·id·ness, ras·cal, rot·ten, rus·tic	/5
Final R	*for	/1
R Blends	brass, crab, craft, crag, cramp, crept, crest, drag, dregs, drift, drill, drop, frills, frog, grab, grin, grit, grunt, strand, strep stress, trap, trip, trot	/24
Multi-Syllable	crim·son, dras·tic, en·**trust**, *for·**bid**·den, fran·tic, fret·ful, grand·est, hun·dred, kes·trel, kin·dred, prob·lem·**at**·ic, pros·pect, traf·fic	/13

* Learned word

Learned Words
from *The Bandit*
by Carolee Dean

Open Syllables Ending in Long Vowels – If these have not been previously taught, introduce them as Learned Words

he, no, she, so, we'll

LEARNED WORDS – Ask students to read the Learned Words list below or use the flashcards. Make a list of words they do not easily recognize and teach them according to the Copy and Memorize procedure. These words are considered "Learned Words" because they must be "learned" by heart either because:

1) They do not follow regular spelling patterns.
2) They are regular but their patterns have not yet been introduced.

*Words that also appear on the target word lists

Learned Words (Irregular)	Learned Words (Not Yet Introduced)
a do into of one the to was	for hope *she *shell *that *them *then what *when *with
/8	/10

Names & Places
from *Gods and Gifts*
by Carolee Dean

Names and Places – Study the names. Create a Vocabulary Foldable.

People and Places	Who or What Are They
Epimetheus (ĕp-ə-MĒ-thē-əs)	one of the Titans
Hephaestus (hə-FĔS-təs)	Greek god of fire and metalworking
Olympus (ō-LĬM-pəs)	home of the Greek gods
Olympians (ō-LĬM-pē-ənz)	the gods who lived on Olympus
Pandora (păn-DOR-ə)	the first human woman
Prometheus (prō-MĒ-thē-əs)	one of the Titans
Titans (TĪ-tənz)	the gods who came before Zeus
Vulcan (VŬL-kən)	the Roman name for Hephaestus
Zeus (zūs)	the king of the Greek gods

Word Cards
from *The Bandit*
by Carolee Dean

Flash Cards – Words on the following pages may be turned into flashcards by cutting them out and gluing them onto index cards OR you may use the card templates and copy them on cardstock before gluing. Make two copies to play card games like Go Fish or the Memory Game. Many of the flashcards are also available for FREE online as Boom Cards at https://wow.boomlearning.com. **Explore Store>Word Travel Press.**

Go Fish – Make a deck of 52 cards by choosing 26 target words. Make two copies of each word and glue the words onto index cards or card stock.
1. Shuffle the cards.
2. Each player receives 7 cards.
3. The rest of the deck is placed face-down on the table.
4. During a turn, a player asks another player for a specific word in their hand. If the second player has the card, they must give it to the first player. That player places the pair face up in front of them and gets a second turn.
5. If the second player does not have that card, they say, "Go Fish," and the first player must choose a card from the deck.
6. The game is over when one player runs out of cards.
7. The winner is the person who has the most pairs of cards.

The Memory Game – Make a deck of 12 cards by choosing 6 target words. Make two copies of each word and glue the words onto index cards or card stock. (Note: Increase the number of cards in increments if the student can handle more cards).
1. Shuffle the cards and place them face down on the table.
2. Each player takes turns turning over 2 cards at a time and reading the words on the cards. If the cards match, the player gets to keep those cards. Do NOT rearrange the remaining cards.
3. The game ends when there are no cards left.
4. The winner is the person who has the most pairs of cards.

Card Template

Playing Cards

Playing Cards

Playing Cards

Playing Cards

Playing Cards

Playing Cards

Word Cards /ă/
from *Gods and Gifts*
by Carolee Dean

an	band
and	bass
ant	bat
as	blast
asp	brass
at	camp
bad	can

Word Cards /ă/

from *Gods and Gifts*
by Carolee Dean

cat	fast
class	gal
crab	grab
craft	grand
crag	had
cramp	ham
drag	jam

Word Cards /ă/

from *Gods and Gifts*
by Carolee Dean

lamp	pad
land	pan
lass	pant
last	pass
man	past
nab	plan
nap	plant

Word Cards /ă/

from *Gods and Gifts*
by Carolee Dean

ran	scalp
rant	scam
rat	scan
sag	slam
sand	spat
scab	strand
scads	swam

Word Cards /ă/

from Gods and Gifts
by Carolee Dean

*that

trap

vast

wax

from *Gods and Gifts*
by Carolee Dean

bell	fed
bend	fell
best	fled
crept	get
den	glen
dress	help
egg	kept

leg	nest
left	pelt
let	pest
melt	red
men	rend
mess	rest
met	send

Word Cards /ĕ/
from *Gods and Gifts*
by Carolee Dean

sent	stem
set	strep
*shell	stress
slept	swept
smell	tell
smelt	*them
sped	*then

Word Cards /ĕ/

from *Gods and Gifts*
by Carolee Dean

web	
wed	
well	
went	
*when	
yen	

41

Word Cards /ĭ/

from *Gods and Gifts*
by Carolee Dean

bit	fill
bliss	fin
cliff	fist
did	fit
dim	flip
drift	frill
drill	gift

Word Cards /ĭ/

from *Gods and Gifts*
by Carolee Dean

glint	hip
grin	hiss
grit	in
hid	it
hill	is
him	lid
hint	lift

Word Cards /ĭ/

limp	pig
lip	pit
lit	rip
milk	silk
mint	sit
	skill
nip	slip

Word Cards /ĭ/

from *Gods and Gifts*
by Carolee Dean

spill	twig
spin	twist
spit	will
split	wilt
swift	wind
tin	*with
trip	

Word Cards /ŏ/

from *Gods and Gifts*
by Carolee Dean

bog	frog
bond	gloss
box	god
dog	got
drop	hog
flop	hop
fox	hot

Word Cards /ŏ/

from *Gods and Gifts*
by Carolee Dean

log	rot
loss	slop
moss	sod
not	spot
on	top
pond	toss
pox	trod

Word Cards /ŏ/

from Gods and Gifts
by Carolee Dean

trot

Word Cards /ŭ/

from *Gods and Gifts*
by Carolee Dean

bluff	hunt
bump	just
but	lump
cut	mud
dusk	mumps
dust	pug
grunt	puss

Word Cards /ŭ/

from *Gods and Gifts*

by Carolee Dean

rust	
slug	
slum	
stuff	
trust	
up	

Two-Syllable

a·**bet**

an·vil

at·tic

ban·dit

bas·set

bliss·ful

bob·cat

bot·tom

can·non

can·yon

com·bat

com·mon

con·flict

Word Cards – Multi-Syllable

from *Gods and Gifts*
by Carolee Dean

con·stant

con·tents

con·vict

crim·son

den·tist

dis·mal

dis·tant

dras·tic

en·**trust**

fal·con

fen·nel

fran·tic

fret·ful

fun·nel

Word Cards – Multi-Syllable

from *Gods and Gifts*
by Carolee Dean

gal·lant

grand·est

help·ful

hid·den

hun·dred

hus·band

ill·ness

in·sult

jac·kal

kin·dred

land·fill

lin·net

mat·tress

pros·pect

Word Cards – Multi-Syllable

from *Gods and Gifts*
by Carolee Dean

pub·lic	sil·ken
pum·mel	sis·kin
rab·bit	sod·den
ras·cal	splen·did
rot·ten	sud·den
rus·tic	sul·len
scan·dal	sum·mit

Word Cards – Multi-Syllable

from *Gods and Gifts*
by Carolee Dean

tem·pest

traf·fic

trod·den

tun·nel

van·dal

ven·om

ves·pid

Vul·can

wist·ful

*with·in

wit·less

Three+ Syllables

dis·con·**tent**·ment

fan·**tas**·tic

*for·**bid**·den

in·**dig**·nant

prob·lem·**at**·tic

rap·id·ness

Word Cards – Suffix -s = /s/

from *Gods and Gifts*
by Carolee Dean

ants	fits
bits	hints
bumps	hips
camps	glints
cats	lamps
drifts	limps
fists	lips

Word Cards - Suffix -s = /s/

from *Gods and Gifts*
by Carolee Dean

lumps	rats
mumps	spits
nests	traps
pants	twists
pests	
pits	
plants	

Word Cards – Suffix -s = /z/

from *Gods and Gifts*
by Carolee Dean

bands	dogs
bells	drills
bogs	eggs
bonds	frills
bugs	glens
bums	gods
dens	grins

Word Cards – Suffix –s = /z/
from *Gods and Gifts*
by Carolee Dean

hills	pads
hogs	pans
jams	plans
lands	ponds
legs	scads
logs	skills
man's	slams

Word Cards – Suffix -s = /z/

from *Gods and Gifts*
by Carolee Dean

slugs

slums

spills

stems

strands

twigs

webs

weds

Word Cards – Multi-Syllable Suffix –s

from *Gods and Gifts*
by Carolee Dean

s = /s/	land·fills
ban·dits	ras·cals
con·tents	scan·dals
con·victs	van·dals
in·sults	
s = /z/	
can·nons	

Word Cards – Final Open Syllable

from *Gods and Gifts*
by Carolee Dean

Directions: If the student does not know these words, teach them as Learned Words using the Strategy of Trace, Copy, Memory.

he

no

she

so

we'll

Word Cards – Irregular Words

from *Gods and Gifts*
by Carolee Dean

Directions: If the student does not know these words, teach them as Learned Words using the Strategy of Trace, Copy, Memory.

a	to
do	was
into	
of	
one	
the	

Word Cards – Pattern Not Yet Learned

from *Gods and Gifts*
by Carolee Dean

Directions: If the student does not know these words, teach them as Learned Words using the Strategy of Trace, Copy, Memory. The ones with * also appear in the target word lists.

for	*then
hope	what
*she	*when
*shell	*with
*that	
*them	

FOUR-IN-A-ROW GAMES

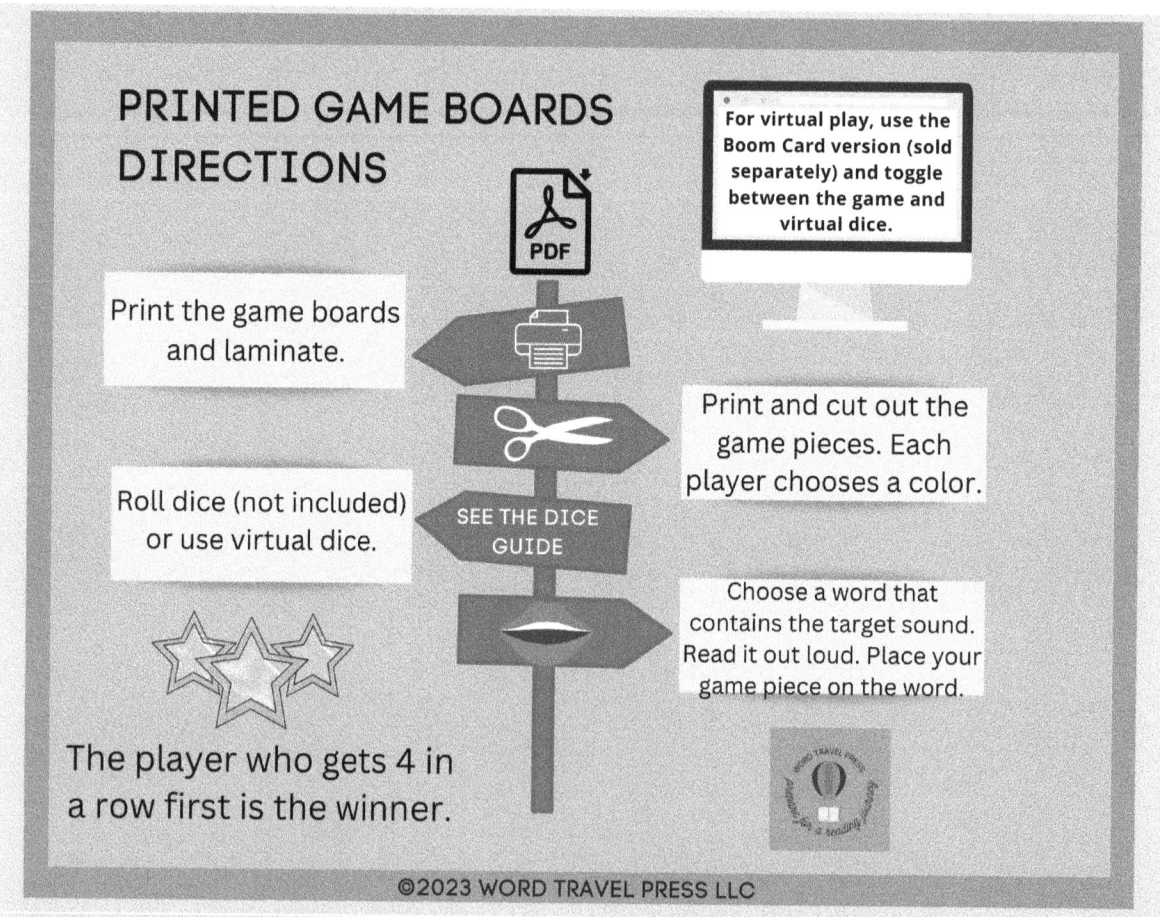

PRINTED GAME BOARDS DIRECTIONS

For virtual play, use the Boom Card version (sold separately) and toggle between the game and virtual dice.

Print the game boards and laminate.

Print and cut out the game pieces. Each player chooses a color.

Roll dice (not included) or use virtual dice.

SEE THE DICE GUIDE

Choose a word that contains the target sound. Read it out loud. Place your game piece on the word.

The player who gets 4 in a row first is the winner.

Dice Key for games 1-8:
1 = a
2 = e
3 = i
4 = o
5 = u
6 = Free

Game 1 = CVC Words
Game 2 = CVC Non-words
Game 3 = CCVC Words
Game 4 = CCVC Non-words
Game 5 = CVCC Words
Game 6 = CVCC Non-words
Game 7 = CCVCC Words
Game 8 = CCVCC Non-words

Dice Key for Game 9: S Words
1 = Initial /s/
2 = Final /s/
3 = Initial /s/ blend
4 = Final /s/ blend
5 = Suffix –s as /s/
6 = s as /z/

Dice Key for Game 10: R Blend Words
1 = CR
2 = DR
3 = TR
4 = GR
5 = FR
6 = STR

Download the PDF. Print. Cut out the game pieces.

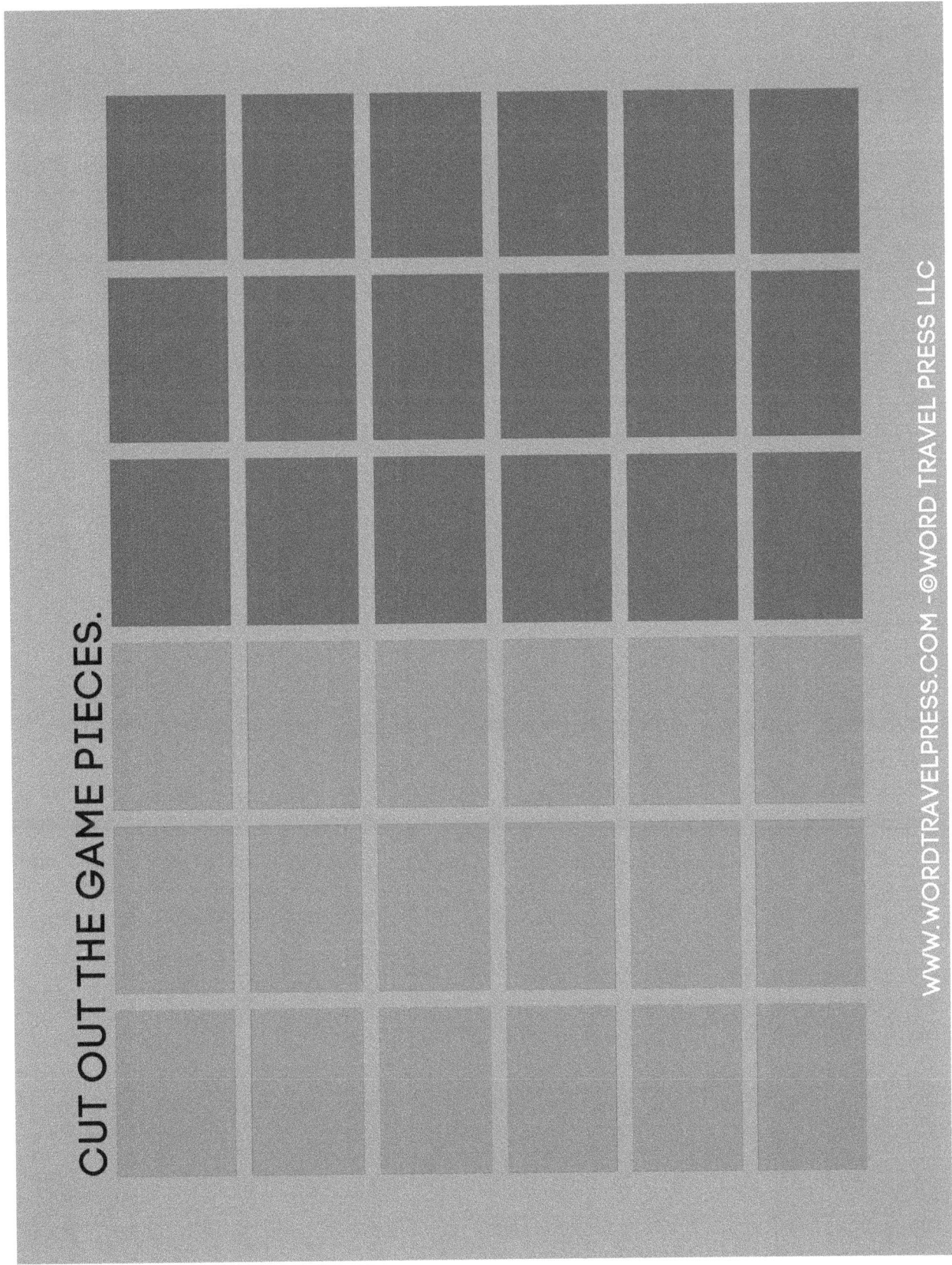

CUT OUT THE GAME PIECES.

WWW.WORDTRAVELPRESS.COM –©WORD TRAVEL PRESS LLC

Download the PDF. Print. Cut out the game pieces.

CUT OUT THE GAME PIECES.

WWW.WORDTRAVELPRESS.COM -©WORD TRAVEL PRESS LLC

4 IN A ROW - CVC

	1	2	3	4	5	6
A	cat	leg	hill	dog	rub	let
B	hog	rat	bed	lip	gill	pup
C	run	fox	bat	cub	rob	pig
D	rim	gut	cod	bass	mess	man
E	fed	fin	pug	get	pass	got

4 IN A ROW - CVC NON-WORDS

	1	2	3	4	5	6
A	cac	lep	hif	dom	rup	lev
B	hob	sas	bep	lif	sim	pud
C	rup	fos	daz	cuv	rom	pim
D	nin	gup	cos	bap	meb	maj
E	feb	fid	puz	fet	gam	gol

4 IN A ROW - CCVC

	1	2	3	4	5	6
A	grab	dwell	drill	stop	drug	fret
B	trot	clap	press	cliff	skin	crux
C	glum	drop	flap	grub	flop	grin
D	flip	flux	frog	crab	step	plan
E	smell	swim	glut	bless	grass	slop

4 IN A ROW - CCVC NON-WORDS

	1	2	3	4	5	6
A	grac	fren	bliz	stob	grum	fren
B	prog	clab	pred	clin	skiv	crum
C	flum	dron	flav	grun	flob	gris
D	flim	gluz	fros	crad	stef	plas
E	cred	swin	clus	blem	grap	slov

4 IN A ROW - CVCC

	1	2	3	4	5	6
A	sand	help	milk	loft	rust	nest
B	pond	gasp	melt	lilt	mist	dust
C	jump	cost	land	hump	lost	hint
D	fist	hunt	romp	pant	tend	rant
E	test	risk	tusk	wept	past	font

WWW.WORDTRAVELPRESS.COM – ©WORD TRAVEL PRESS LLC

4 IN A ROW - CVCC
NON-WORDS

	1	2	3	4	5	6
A	sant	ject	milp	cond	tund	nesk
B	pont	gast	melz	lisk	miln	dunt
C	junt	cosp	lant	hust	ponz	hilk
D	fimp	hund	ront	pand	tect	rand
E	tesk	rist	tust	wext	palp	fomp

4 IN A ROW - CCVCC

	1	2	3	4	5	6
A	grand	crept	flint	frond	stunt	slept
B	stomp	blast	swept	skimp	clomp	stump
C	crust	frost	stand	clump	crimp	stilt
D	glint	grunt	blond	plant	spent	grant
E	cleft	crisp	trust	crest	craft	tromp

4 IN A ROW - CCVCC
NON-WORDS

#8

	1	2	3	4	5	6
A	dramp	drept	glimp	grond	spunt	stelp
B	slont	brast	swelm	stimp	cromp	slund
C	drusk	fromp	frand	crunt	drimt	spist
D	flind	flunt	blont	plast	slent	blant
E	sleft	crint	brust	cremp	braft	trond

4 IN A ROW - S: 1 = INITIAL S, 2 = FINAL S, 3 = INITIAL S BLEND, 4= FINAL S BLEND, 5 = SUFFIX S AS /S/, 6 = S AS /Z/

	1	2	3	4	5	6
A	sag	brass	skill	best	ants	bands
B	bells	send	class	slam	box	bumps
C	fits	dogs	set	dress	stop	blast
D	pest	hints	hills	sit	mess	swept
E	spin	rust	traps	pans	so	pass

4 IN A ROW - R BLENDS

#10

1 = CR S, 2 = DR, 3 = TR, 4= GR, 5 = FR, 6 = STR

	1	2	3	4	5	6
A	craft	drag	trip	grit	strep	frill
B	frog	cramp	drop	trap	grin	stress
C	strand	fret	crept	dress	trot	grunt
D	grab	strap	frost	crest	drill	trust
E	trend	grip	strip	frond	crag	drift

DICTATION

/ă/ Words

based on *Gods and Gifts*
by Carolee Dean

Directions: The following sentences may be used for dictation, spelling, articulation, and/or reading practice. Questions are used so that students can practice final punctuation more deliberately.

Word	Sentence
1. past	Tad had a sad past.
2. sand	Dan sat in the sand.
3. band	Jan is in a brass band.
4. spam	Dad had spam and ham.
5. wax	Did Pam wax the van?
6. camp	Did the camp bag sag?
7. plant	Did Cam plant grass?
8. grab	Did Fran grab the jam?
9. rant	Sam is on a rant.
10. class	Brad had a rat in class.

/10

DICTATION

/ĕ/ Words

based on *Gods and Gifts*
by Carolee Dean

Directions: The following sentences may be used for dictation, spelling, articulation, and/or reading practice.

Word	Sentence
1. dress	Did Jess get a dress?
2. test	Will Ted pass the test?
3. rest	Can Tex rest on the bed?
4. send	Did Jan send it?
5. stem	Is the stem red?
6. swept	Fred swept up the mess.
7. went	Jeb went in a cab.
8. fled	Ben fled in a van.
9. left	Sam left the bag.
10. slept	Dad slept in the den.

/10

DICTATION

/ĭ/ Words

based on *Gods and Gifts*
by Carolee Dean

Directions: The following sentences may be used for dictation, spelling, articulation, and/or reading practice.

Word	Sentence
1. cliff	Bill is up on the cliff.
2. silk	Jill has a silk dress.
3. skill	Jim had a lot of skill.
4. slip	Did Sid slip in the pit?
5. spit	Did Will spit on it?
6. swift	The wind is swift.
7. gift	The gift is in the bag.
8. trip	Will went on a trip.
9. twig	Did the twig snap?
10. grin	Can a cat grin?

/10

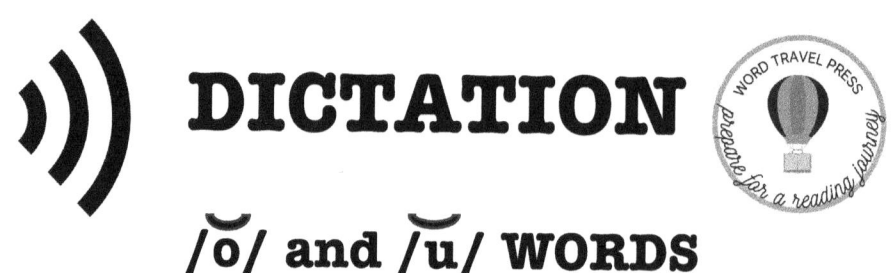

DICTATION

/ŏ/ and /ŭ/ WORDS

based on *Gods and Gifts*
by Carolee Dean

Directions: The following sentences may be used for dictation, spelling, articulation, and/or reading practice.

Word	Sentence
1. spot	The dress had a spot on it.
2. stop	Will Bob stop the plan?
3. dusk	Gus will run at dusk.
4. dust	Is the dust in the cup?
5. trust	Mom did not trust him.
6. stuff	The rest of the stuff is in the bag.
7. bluff	Did the men go up on the bluff?
8. pond	Is the bug in the pond?
9. trod	The pig trod on the log.
10. bond	Did the pals bond?

/10

PHONOLOGICAL AWARENESS

INTRODUCTION

Phonological Awareness is one of the foundational Components of Reading (COR). Learn more about this important skill on the COR INSTRUCTION page at https://wordtravelpress.com/.

Phonological awareness includes rhyming, counting syllables, and detecting initial, final, and medial sounds or phonemes. Prosody has also been included which involves recognizing the suprasegmental features of words such as rhythm, stress, pitch, and intonation.

Phonemic awareness is the part of phonological awareness that deals specifically with individual sounds. Students work with syllables and phonemes in the following activities by isolating, segmenting, adding, deleting, and substituting.

Phonemic skills are first taught as an oral skill (without letters) in the oral exercises found in the **Say It Again, Sam** activity. But phonemic awareness has the greatest impact when sounds are paired with letters and integrated with writing and spelling (Paulson, 2018 p. 234). In the **Sound Tracks** activity, students change one sound at a time to create new words. In **Rhyme Time** they work with the concepts of rhyme and alliteration with the added component of writing a sentence containing an alliteration. In **Feel the Beat**, students identify the stressed syllables in a line of poetry. In the **Dictation** activity in the previous section, students draw upon their knowledge of sound-letter correspondences to write short sentences to dictation. The sentences in **Dictation** may also be used for reading practice.

Activities are described in more detail below:

Say It Again, Sam—Students work on deletion by repeating words and leaving out sounds or syllables. They start by deleting the first syllable from a two-syllable word. Next, they delete the second syllable. Then, they delete the initial sounds, final sounds, and medial sounds. The medial sounds are parts of consonant blends. They are more difficult to isolate than single consonants. In this way, students move from more basic to more challenging phonological and phoneme awareness activities.

For a deeper and much more extensive exploration of phoneme awareness, see *Equipped for Reading Success: A Comprehensive, Step-By-Step Program for Developing Phonemic Awareness and Fluent Word Recognition* by David Kilpatrick.

See the following page for additional phonological awareness activities.

Continued

Feel the Beat, students underline the stressed words in lines of a poem. Then they read the poem by exaggerating the underlined words. They do this by saying the stressed syllables longer, louder, and with a slightly higher pitch. Next, they incorporate two-syllable words and draw drumsticks above the stressed syllable. Finally, they read the poems with normal stress. Ask them if they can still feel the beat. If not, instruct them to try reading the poem like a robot, giving every word the same stress. Then read the poem again with stress on the highlighted syllables to bring out the difference.

In *Rhyme Time #1 and 2,* students circle words that rhyme and underline alliterations (words that start with the same sound). They then create a sentence that uses alliteration. This process also helps them understand and use literary devices. Additionally, switching between these three tasks requires students to use cognitive flexibility at both the letter-sound and meaning levels. Some students may not be ready to switch between tasks. For them, do one task at a time. For a metacognitive activity, ask students to think about how they tackle tasks. Would they rather complete all three steps for each target word before moving on OR would they prefer to do all the rhymes first, then all the alliterations, and then all the sentences? Get them talking about their internal processes and preferences.

In **Rhyme Time #3-5**, students fill in the blanks with words (or parts of two-syllable words) that fit the poem. In **Rhyme Time #6**, students create their own poems. This activity can be much more challenging than it appears, so students may benefit from working with partners. Complete an example poem as a class before asking students to tackle this on their own.

Advanced students may be interested in a discussion of rhythm and meter. The excerpt from *The Bandit* in Feel the Beat #2, as well as Rhyme Time #5 are all written in trochaic tetrameter. Lines occasionally start with an added unstressed beat or end on a stressed beat, but the overall stress pattern is trochaic, meaning the stress on the first syllable of a "foot" or set. This is the DUH-duh pattern. Examples of trochee can be found in words like **ti**ger, **can**dle, **slee**ping. Tetrameter refers to the fact that there are four sets or feet of trochee in each line of verse. Understanding patterns of stressed and unstressed syllables in poetry is an advanced application of phonological awareness.

Tro**cha**ic Tetrameter = **DUH**-duh, **DUH**-duh, **DUH**-duh, **DUH**-duh
Twinkle **Twin**kle **Lit**tle **Star**

References:

Kilpatrick, D.A. (2016). Equipped for reading success: A comprehensive, step-by-step program for developing phonemic awareness and fluent word recognition. Syracuse, NY: Casey & Kirsch Publishers.

Paulson, L. H. (2018). Teaching phonemic awareness. In J.R. Birsh & S. Carreker (Eds.) *Multisensory teaching of basic language skills* (4th ed., pp. 205-253). Baltimore, MD: Paul H. Brookes Publishing Co.

Say It Again, Sam
Two-Syllable Words

Initial Syllable Deletion
based on *The Bandit*
by Carolee Dean

Directions:
The teacher says a two-syllable word. The student repeats the word. The teacher says which syllable to delete. The student says the syllable that is left. Note that the stress in the first three words is on the second syllable.

Teacher	student	Teacher	Student
Say….		Say it again but leave out…	
abet	abet	/uh/	bet
entrust	entrust	/en/	trust
forbid	forbid	/for/	bid
helpful	helpful	/help/	full
wistful	wistful	/wist/	full
rustic	rustic	/rus/	tic
prospect	prospect	/pros/	pect
frantic	frantic	/fran/	tic
summit	summit	/sum/	it
blissful	blissful	/blis/	full

/10

Say It Again, Sam
Two-Syllable Words

Final Syllable Deletion
based on *The Bandit*
by Carolee Dean

Directions:
The teacher says a two-syllable word. The student repeats the word. The teacher says which syllable to delete. The student says the syllable that is left. Note that the stress in the initial word is on the first syllable.

Teacher	student	Teacher	Student
Say….		Say it again but leave out…	
bandit	**bandit**	/dit/	**ban**
crimson	**crimson**	/zn/	**crim**
canyon	**canyon**	/yun/	**can**
dismal	**dismal**	/mul/	**diz**
distant	**distant**	/tunt/	**dis**
Vulcan	**Vulcan**	/kun/	**vul**
rascal	**rascal**	/cul/	**ras**
frantic	**frantic**	/tic/	**fran**
hundred	**hundred**	/dred/	**hun**
anvil	**anvil**	/vul/	**an**

/10

Say It Again, Sam
One-Syllable Words

Initial /s/ Sound Deletion in Blends
based on *The Bandit*
by Carolee Dean

Directions: The teacher says the word. The student repeats the word. The teacher says which sound to delete. The student says what is left. Tell the student that some (but not all) will result in real words.

Teacher	student	Teacher	Student
Say....		Say it again but leave out...	
slip	**slip**	/s/	**lip**
skill	**skill**	/s/	**kill**
smelt	**smelt**	/s/	**melt**
sped	**sped**	/s/	**ped**
spit	**spit**	/s/	**pit**
spot	**spot**	/s/	**pot**
stuff	**stuff**	/s/	**tuff**
swept	**swept**	/s/	**wept**
swift	**swift**	/s/	**wift**
stop	**stop**	/s/	**top**

/10

Say It Again, Sam
One-Syllable Words

Final Sound Deletion
based on *The Bandit*
by Carolee Dean

Directions: The teacher says the word. The student repeats the word. The teacher says which sound to delete. The student says what is left. Some may be non-words.

Teacher	student	Teacher	Student
Say….		Say it again but leave out…	
band	band	/d/	ban
camp	camp	/p/	cam
smelt	smelt	/t/	smell
crest	crest	/t/	cress
swift	swift	/t/	swiff
silk	silk	/k/	sill
bond	bond	/d/	bon
pond	pond	/d/	pon
trust	trust	/t/	truss
dusk	dusk	/k/	duss

/10

Say It Again, Sam
One-Syllable Words

Medial /s/ Sound Deletion
based on *The Bandit*
by Carolee Dean

Directions: The teacher says the word. The student repeats the word. The teacher says which sound to delete. The student says what is left. Some may be non-words

Teacher	student	Teacher	Student
Say….		Say it again but leave out…	
crest	**crest**	/s/	**cret**
dusk	**dusk**	/s/	**duck**
dust	**dust**	/s/	**dut**
fast	**fast**	/s/	**fat**
past	**past**	/s/	**pat**
last	**last**	/s/	**lat**
rest	**rest**	/s/	**ret**
vast	**vast**	/s/	**vat**
trust	**trust**	/s/	**trut**
crust	**crust**	/s/	**crut**

/10

SOUND TRACKS
based on *Gods and Gifts*
by Carolee Dean

Directions: The teacher says the first word. The student repeats the word and uses the Sound Tracks Letters at this end of this section to construct the word saying each sound. The student then reads the entire word. The teacher then says another word with one sound changed. The student says the new word, makes the sound change saying each sound, then reads the entire word. Some of the words may be non-words. Letters are also available for FREE on Boom Cards.

List 1 – Initial /s/ blends	List 2 – Final /s/ blends	List 3 – /nd/ Blends	List 4 - /nt/ blends
slip	fast	and	ant
stip	vast	band	pant
strip	past	rand	plant
strap	last	trand	lant
strop	list	strand	rant
stop	wist	stand	grant
slop	twist	sand	gant
slot	twust	send	glant
spot	trust	spend	glint
pot	rust	pend	hint
pet	dust	tend	hunt
ept	dest	trend	tunt
wept	rest	rend	stunt
swept	crest	end	sunt
slept	crust	bend	punt

/45

SOUND TRACKS
Letters
based on *Level 1 of the HOT ROD Series*
by Carolee Dean

Directions: Cut out the letters below to use for the Sound Tracks Activity. Enlarge as needed and glue onto card stock to make them easier to pick up. A digital version of the activity may be found for FREE at Boom **Learning** at https://wow.boomlearning.com. Explore **Store>Word Travel Press.**

a	e	i	o	u

b	c	d	f	g	h	j	k	l	m

n	p	r	s	t	v	w	x	y	z

Feel the Beat #1
based on *No Gift for Man*
by Carolee Dean

Directions: Read the lines of poetry below.
1. Underline each stressed beat following the pattern in the first line.
2. Read this segment of the poem and exaggerate the stressed words.
3. Read the lines of poetry again, but this time in your normal voice.
4. Can you still feel the beat?

Excerpt from *No Gift for Man* (Set 1, Book 1 – The HOT ROD series)

A <u>gift</u> for the <u>dog</u>.
A gift for the cat.

A gift for the hog.
A gift for the rat.

The frog got a hop.
The bass got a fin.

The <u>bat</u> can <u>drop</u>.
The drill can grin.

The fox can hunt.
The pug can smell.

The pig got a grunt.
The crab got a shell.

Feel the Beat #1
based on *No Gift for Man*
by Carolee Dean

ANSWERS

Excerpt from No Gift for Man (Set 1, Book 1 – The HOT ROD series)

A <u>gift</u> for the <u>dog</u>.
A <u>gift</u> for the <u>cat</u>.

A <u>gift</u> for the <u>hog</u>.
A <u>gift</u> for the <u>rat</u>.

The <u>frog</u> got a <u>hop</u>.
The <u>bass</u> got a <u>fin</u>.

The <u>bat</u> can <u>drop</u>.
The <u>drill</u> can <u>grin</u>.

The <u>fox</u> can <u>hunt</u>.
The <u>pug</u> can <u>smell</u>.

The <u>pig</u> got a <u>grunt</u>.
The <u>crab</u> got a <u>shell</u>.

Feel the Beat #2
based on *The Bandit*
by Carolee Dean

Directions: Read the lines of poetry below.
1. Draw a drumstick above each stressed beat. Follow the pattern in the first line.
2. Read the poem and tap the stressed words with a pencil or drumstick.
3. Read the lines of poetry again, but this time in your normal voice.
4. Can you still feel the beat?

Excerpt from *The Bandit* (Level 1 – The HOT ROD series)

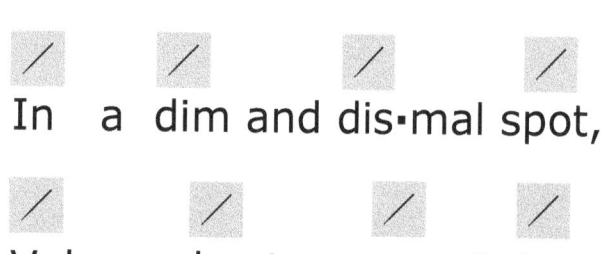

In   a dim and dis·mal spot,

Vul·can kept an an·vil hot.

A ban·dit crept in with a plan

to get a help·ful gift for man.

He hid it in a fen·nel stem.

Will Vul ·can pelt and pum·mel him?

94

Feel the Beat #2
based on *The Bandit*
by Carolee Dean

ANSWERS

In   a dim and dis·mal spot,

Vul·can kept an an·vil hot.

A ban·dit crept in with a plan

to get a help·ful gift for man.

He hid it in a fen · nel stem.

Will Vul ·can pelt and pum ·mel him?

Rhyme Time #1
based on *No Gift for Man*
by Carolee Dean

Directions: Read the target words below, and then:
1. Circle words that rhyme with it.
2. Underline words that start with the same sound. This is called *alliteration*.
3. Use the target word and a word that starts with the same sound to write a sentence. Use another piece of paper if needed.

1. dog	(hog)	<u>dug</u>	rot	(blog)	<u>dig</u>
	Sentence:	The <u>dog</u> <u>dug</u> in the mud.			
2. rat	rug	asp	bat	sat	man
	Sentence:				
3. fin	hop	spin	fat	skin	fill
	Sentence:				
4. cat	can	bug	hat	cut	spat
	Sentence:				
5. drill	drop	flip	skill	drum	bill
	Sentence:				
6. grin	win	grab	mat	grit	punt
	Sentence:				
7. hunt	pig	grunt	hat	hid	stunt
	Sentence:				
8. trot	hot	trip	sand	trap	spot
	Sentence:				

Rhyme Time #1
based on *No Gift for Man*
by Carolee Dean

ANSWERS

Sentence content will vary

Rhymes - 15, Alliterations – 15 = 30 Total

1. dog	(hog)	dug	rot	(blog)	dig
2. rat	rug	asp	(bat)	(sat)	man
3. fin	hop	(spin)	fat	(skin)	fill
4. cat	can	bug	(hat)	cut	(spat)
5. drill	drop	flip	(skill)	drum	(bill)
6. grin	(win)	grab	mat	grit	punt
7. hunt	pig	(grunt)	hat	hid	(stunt)
8. trot	(hot)	trip	sand	trap	(spot)

Rhyme Time #2
based on *The Bandit*
by Carolee Dean

Directions: Read the target words below, and then:
1. Circle words that rhyme with it.
2. Underline words that start with the same sound. This is called *alliteration*.
3. Use the target word and a word that starts with the same sound to write a sentence. Use another piece of paper if needed.

1. band	(hand)	bag	pit	(land)	big
	Sentence:	The band had a big bag of buns.			

2. crest	crept	rest	crab	crust	jest
	Sentence:				

3. drift	hug	gift	drag	drum	lift
	Sentence:				

4. bond	pond	bog	fond	band	glen
	Sentence:				

5. trust	trip	dust	must	trap	sped
	Sentence:				

6. stop	Step	hop	stem	web	flop
	Sentence:				

7. slip	hint	trip	hip	slump	slop
	Sentence:				

8. melt	pelt	smelt	met	felt	men
	Sentence:				

Rhyme Time #2
based on *The Bandit*
by Carolee Dean

ANSWERS

Sentence content will vary
Rhymes - 17, Alliterations – 17 = 34 Total

1. band	(hand)	bag	pit	(land)	big
2. crest	crept	(rest)	crab	crust	(jest)
3. drift	hug	(gift)	drag	drum	(lift)
4. bond	(pond)	bog	(fond)	band	glen
5. trust	trip	(dust)	(must)	trap	sped
6. stop	step	(hop)	stem	web	(flop)
7. slip	hint	(trip)	(hip)	slump	slop
8. melt	(pelt)	(smelt)	met	(felt)	men

Rhyme Time #3
based on *No Gift for Man*
by Carolee Dean

Directions:
1. Insert words into blank boxes to complete the poem below.
2. For two syllable words use two boxes (one per syllable).
3. Read the finished poem out loud adding stress to the words with stars.

The	*		*had	a	*cat.
The	*	cat	*had	a	*rat.
The	*	rat	*had	a	*grin,
And	*		*on	his	*chin.

Example:.
The **ban-dit** had a cat.
The **fat** cat had a rat.
The **smug** rat had a grin,
And **muf-fin** on his chin.

Rhyme Time #4
based on *No Gift for Man*
by Carolee Dean

Directions:
1. Fill in the blanks below to create your own poem.
2. Rhyming words have been provided, or you can cross them out and write your own rhyming words above.
3. Fill in the blank boxes with words (or parts of two-syllable words) that fit the poem.
4. Boxes with stars should be stressed.
5. Boxes should only contain one syllable.
6. Read the finished poem out loud and stress the words with stars.
7. Make changes if needed and read your poem out loud again.

	*		*		*bat

	*		*		*hat

	*		*		*den

	*		*		*pen

Rhyme Time #5
based on *The Bandit*
by Carolee Dean

Directions:
1. Write words in blank boxes to complete the poem.
2. For two-syllable words, use two boxes.
3. Read the finished poem out loud.
4. Use the eraser end of your pencil to tap the words that have drumsticks, These are stressed syllables.

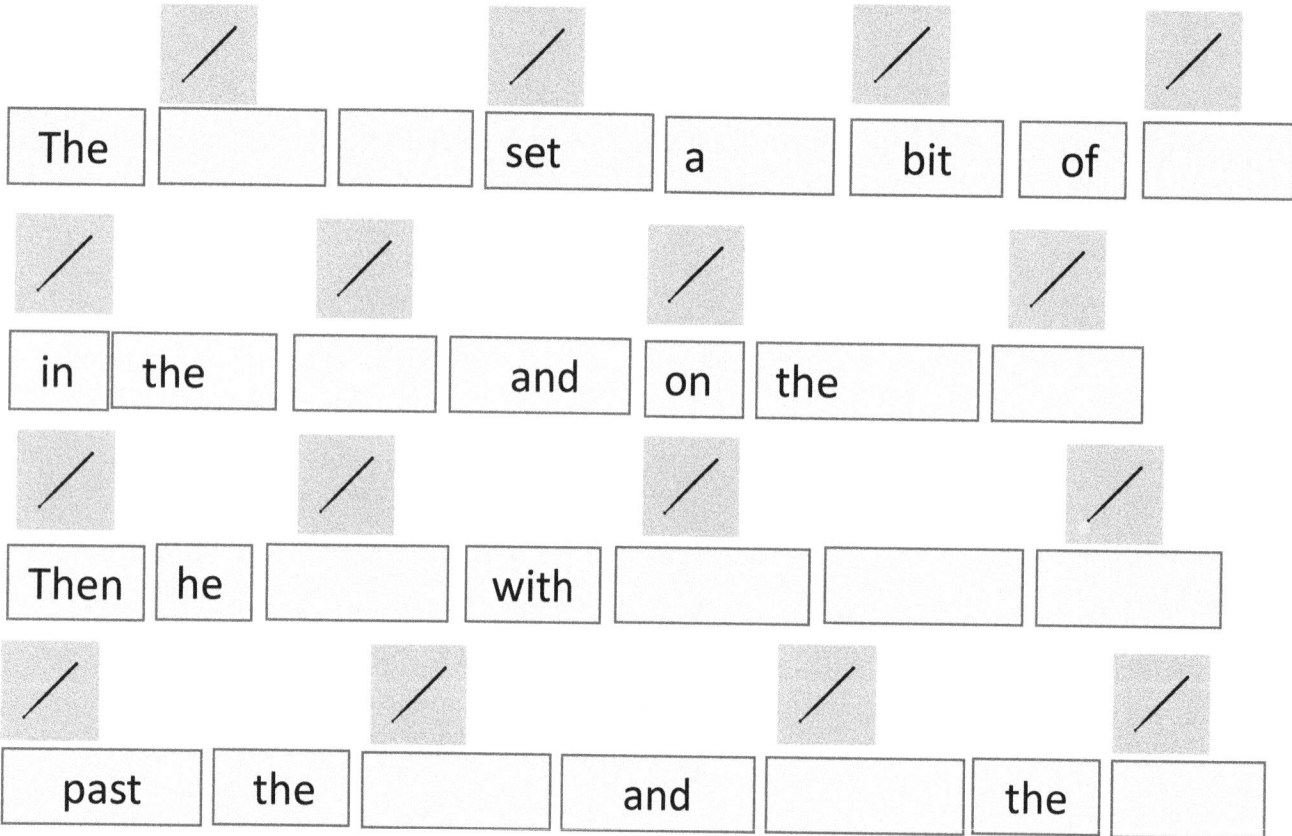

Example:.
The **ban**-dit **set** a **bit** of **sand**
in the **pits** and **on** the **land**.
Then he **ran** with **wit** and **skill**
past the **gods** and **up** the **hill**.

Rhyme Time #6
based on *Gods and Gifts*
by Carolee Dean

Directions:
1. Write a pair of words that rhyme with each other in the A boxes.
2. Write a different pair of words that rhyme with each other in the B boxes.
3. Write words in the rest of the empty boxes to make a poem.
4. For two-syllable words, use two boxes.
5. Read the finished poem out loud.
6. Use the eraser end of your pencil to tap the words that have drumsticks. These are stressed syllables.

Rhyme Pair Examples: can, pan; cat, bat; band, land; rest, best; stop, hop; felt, melt; gift, lift; must, dust; trip, slip

Cognitive Flexibility

INTRODUCTION

What is Cognitive Flexibility

Cognitive flexibility is an important executive function skill that centers on the ability to switch between different types of information. It can involve switching between different tasks or thinking about more than one concept at a time. Working memory is an important element of cognitive flexibility that helps a person manage more than one task, concept, or piece of information at the same time. It impacts reading, writing, spelling, and more.

How Cognitive Flexibility Impacts Reading

Specific to reading, cognitive flexibility is essential for both decoding and comprehension. Students need cognitive flexibility to be able to hold different possible pronunciations for a letter or combination of letters in mind while decoding unfamiliar words. At the same time, they must consider the word's meaning. Working memory enables a reader to compare the possible pronunciations of a word with words in their lexicon (internal dictionary). While they are figuring out how to pronounce the word and determining what the word means, a reader must also hold the rest of the sentence in mind. The content and structure of the sentence will also affect the meaning of the word. If a word has multiple meanings, cognitive flexibility is required to hold the possible options in short-term memory while making judgments about the best fit within the context of the sentence and paragraph.

While many tasks are useful for developing cognitive flexibility, not many directly relate to reading and decoding. The activities on the next few pages were designed to address executive function skills that directly relate to a structured literacy scope and sequence. By sorting words that belong to two different categories simultaneously, students can work on cognitive flexibility.

Cognitive Flexibility

For more information about Cognitive Flexibility as well as a FREE printable activity based on Level 1 of the HOT ROD series (CVC, CCVC, CVCC, CCCVC, etc), visit the Cognitive Flexibility Page at www.wordtravelpress.com.

The *Cognitive Flexibility Category Sorts & Multiple Classification Tasks* for *Closed Syllables* is a 38- page PDF filled with lists containing closed syllable words that can be cut out and sorted according to a variety of categories.

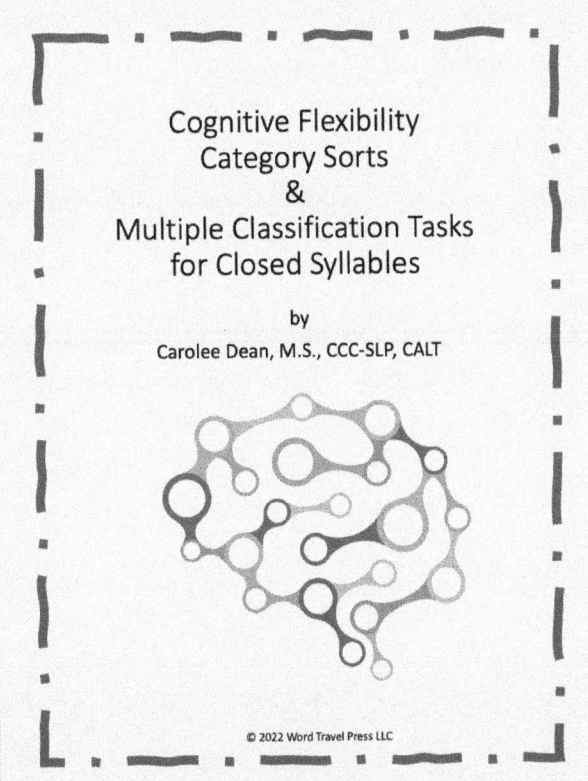

Cognitive Flexibility
Category Sorts
&
Multiple Classification Tasks
for Closed Syllables

by

Carolee Dean, M.S., CCC-SLP, CALT

© 2022 Word Travel Press LLC

Cognitive Flexibility Online Game

In addition to the printable resource on the previous page, A FREE Digital Boom Card activity is available online. See the Downloadable Resources page near the end of the book for details or go to https://wow.boomlearning.com and explore Store>Word Travel Press. Additional digital resources are available on that page. Some are free and some have an additional charge.

The target words in the free online Boom game are: fox, claps, dogs, pigs, drops, pups, spits, swims, spins, runs, cubs, cats

This digital Boom Deck has three component parts:
1. First students sort words into two categories: Animals & Actions.
2. Next, they sort the SAME cards into two different categories: the final /s/ sound and the final /z/ sound.
   (Note: reproducible activities for these category sorts are also available on the next two pages.)
3. Finally, students sort the same words on a 2x2 matrix while considering all 4 categories at once.

This sorting activity is based on a Cognitive Flexibility study conducted by Carolee Dean and Kelly Cartwright, Ph.D. For additional information, contact info@wordtravelpress.com.

References:
Cartwright, K.B. (2023). _Executive skills and reading comprehension: A guide for educators_ (Second Edition). New York, NY: Guildford Press.

Tunmer, W.E., & Chapman, J.W. (2012). Does set for variability mediate the influence of vocabulary knowledge on the development of word recognition skills? _Scientific Studies of Reading_, 16(2), 122-140.

Vadasy, P.F., Sanders, E.A., Cartwright, K.B. (2022). Cognitive flexibility in beginning decoding and encoding. _The Journal of Education for Students Placed at Risk_, in press.

Zipke, M. (2016). The importance of flexibility of pronunciation in learning to decode: A training study in set for variability. _First Language_. 36 (1), 71-86.

Cognitive Flexibility

Category Sort
Animals vs. Actions

Directions: Cut out the words and place them in the correct category.

fox	pigs	spits	runs
claps	drops	swims	cubs
dogs	pups	spins	cats

Animals   Actions

Cognitive Flexibility
Category Sort
Final /s/ Sound vs. Final /z/ Sound

Directions: Cut out the words and place them in the correct category.

fox	pigs	spits	runs
claps	drops	swims	cubs
dogs	pups	spins	cats

/s/   /z/

Cognitive Flexibility

Start with the sorting activities on the previous two pages to prepare for the Multiple Classification Activity below. You will need a Boom Learning account to play the game online or you may copy and cut out the words on the previous pages and create your own 2x2 grid. You may sign up for a free Boom Account at www.wow.boomlearning.com. Additional CF activities are available there for a small additional charge. Strategies for students who need help with this task are on the next page.

Below is a sample of the Multiple Classification Task. Observe that there are two ANIMALS and one ACTION. Therefore, an ACTION is needed for B1.

There are two FINAL /s/ words and one FINAL /z/ word, therefore a /z/ word is needed for B1.

B1 must be an ACTION that ends with the /z/ sound. There are three possible answers.

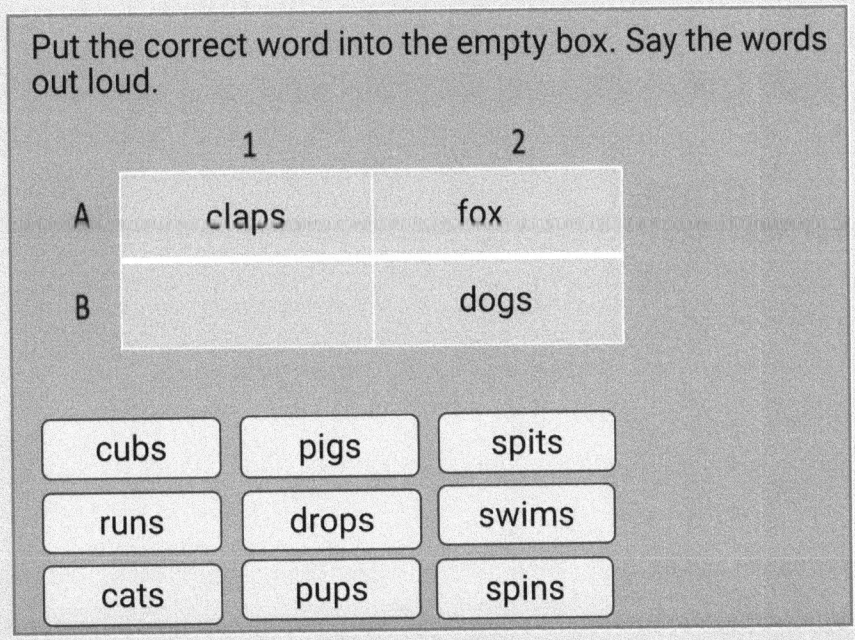

Answers: runs, swims, spins

Cognitive Flexibility

SODAS Strategy

S = Study
O = Observe
D = Deduce
A = Assess and Add
S = Select

Students who need more explicit instruction to be successful with the 2x2 matrix may benefit from the SODAS Strategy below.

Put the correct word into the empty box to complete the set. Use the **SODAS** strategy if you need help to decide which word to choose.

	1	2
A	fox	spits
B	dogs	

cubs

runs

drops

1. **Study** the words.

2. **Observe** that Row A contains 2 /s/ words. Row B contains 1 /z/ word.

3. **Deduce** that Row B is missing a /z/ word.

4. Observe that column 1 contains two kinds of animals. Column 2 contains one action.

5. Deduce that Column 2 is missing an action.

6. **Assess and Add** the two missing elements. B2 needs to be a final /z/ word and an action.

7. **Select** a word that fits the pattern. **You may write down the 2 missing elements if that helps.**

Answer: runs

MORPHOLOGY

INTRODUCTION

While phonemes represent the smallest units of sound, morphemes represent the smallest units of meaning. English is a morphophonemic language which means that the phonemes and the morphological structure work together to affect how words are pronounced.

In her chapter on "Morphology for Reading, Spelling, and Vocabulary," in *Speech to Print: Language Essentials for Teachers* (Third Edition), Louisa Moats talks about the power of morphological awareness for building vocabulary. Being able to recognize morphemes enhances a student's ability to make reasonable inferences about a word's meaning in context. That recognition and understanding helps to "anchor a word in memory." In addition, we remember words best when we understand their relationship to other words.

Moats provides guidelines for morphology development and provides a scope and sequence for instruction based on the three layers of language: Ango-Saxon, Latin, and Greek in that order. Using her framework, the examples found in *Gods and Gifts* appear in **bold** below. As you choose morphology activities for your students, consider what they are ready to tackle in this sequence. Also, consider their decoding abilities and if they have been introduced previously to the affixes. The activities in this section are organized using Moats' scope and sequence.

Anglo-Saxon (common things and actions like ***dog, land, cat, man, help, rest, trust***)
1. Compound words like ***bobcat, landfill.***
2. High-frequency prefixes added to Anglo-Saxon base words (****en, *dis,*** un, mis)
3. Common suffixes added to base words that do not cause spelling changes (***–s,*** -ed, -ing)
4. Other suffixes that begin with a consonant (***-ness, -less, -ful, -ment***)
5. Other suffixes that begin with a vowel (**-*en**) Vowel suffixes that require changes in the base word because of the doubling, dropping, or changing rule (**hidden, trodden**).

Latin
1. Prefixes that end in a consonant or vowel-r (***non, con, ex, *dis,*** per)
2. Prefixes that end in a vowel (****pro,*** re)
3. Two-syllable prefixes (*intro*)
4. Roots such as ***vict*** (conquer), **flict** (strike), ***bat*** (fight), ***dent*** (tooth), **mal** (*bad*), ***tent*** (to hold), ***spect*** (see)
5. Assimilated prefixes like ***com*** (from con)
6. Suffixes (*-ion as in tion, -able, -ive, -or*)

Greek
1. Combining forms such as *micro, scope, bio, logy,* ***pro, epi, pan***

*Note: **En** can be a prefix or suffix, but it means different things. Many Latin affixes such as **dis** are also used with Anglo-Saxon base words. **Pro** has both Greek and Latin origins.

MORPHOLOGY

Continued (page 2)

Morpho Mania #1 – Compound Words (all three stories)
Create compound words to complete a fill-in-the-blank activity.

Morpho Mania #2: Suffix –s Meaning (all three stories)
Suffix -s has several meanings when added to the end of a word. It can signal the possessive (Pam's cat), plural (three cats), or action (He swims). The meaning is based how words are used in a sentence (He walks to school; She goes for walks on weekdays). In this activity, students read the sentence and decide if suffix –s is signifying possessive, plural, or action.

Morpho Mania #3: Suffix – s Sounds (all three stories)
Suffix –s can sound like /s/ (cats, Jack's, walks) or /z/ (dogs, Meg's, jogs). In this activity, students sort words containing suffix –s based on the final sound. The focus on sound endings makes this activity a phonological exercise as well as a morphological one. If students have difficulty telling the difference between /s/ and /z/, they may benefit from a discussion about voiced versus unvoiced sounds. Prompt them to place a hand on their throat and feel the vibration of /z/. Notice how the /z/ and /s/sounds are made the same way in the mouth, except that /z/ is voiced. They can also study the letter just before suffix –s. If that sound is voiced (/b/, /d/, /g/, /l/, /m/, /n/ /r/, /v/) then suffix –s will be a voiced /z/. If the sound is unvoiced, (/k/, /f/, /p/, /t/) then suffix –s will be an unvoiced /s/.

Morphology #4: Suffixes *ful, ness, less*(*The Bandit* and *The Box*)
ful means "full of"
ness means "having the essence or quality of"
less means "without"
The suffixes in activity #4 are all consonant suffixes because they start with a consonant. They don't affect the spelling of a base word the way that vowel suffixes can. They are also easily decodable. However, they may be tricky to spell. Students might expect *ful* to be spelled like the word *full*. If students have learned that the floss rule applies to stressed syllables, then spelling *ness* and *less* may also be a challenge. For this reason, the morphology activities focus on reading rather than spelling. Although both *restless* and *restlessness* are defined, only restless appears in the game cards; however, this could be a good opportunity to talk about how suffixes can change parts of speech

rest – noun, verb   *restless* – adjective   *restlessness* - noun

MORPHOLOGY

Continued (page 3)

Morpho Mania #5: Suffix –EN (*The Bandit*)
This is a vowel suffix because it starts with a vowel. This makes the base word subject to several spelling rules (doubling, dropping, changing). Students may not yet have learned these rules. Some of the words chosen for this activity incorporate the doubling rule. Students should be able to read words following this rule even if they are not ready to spell them. Suffix –*EN* affects meaning in several ways - a) changing a noun to an adjective – silk to silken, b) changing an adjective to a verb – glad to gladden, c) signifying that a verb is a past participle and that an action has been completed (was stolen). Past participles may also be used as adjectives (We found the stolen car.) Students can benefit from studying the words and definitions, even if they are not ready to study the various purposes of suffix –*en*.

Morpho Mania #6: Prefix Pro (all three stories)
The focus of words for Level 1 is on closed sounds with a few open syllable words (he, no, so). The prefix PRO ends in a vowel, so some students may not be ready for this activity or may need instruction on how to pronounce words with this prefix. All words selected contain closed syllable roots with the exception of *pronouns*. Discuss with students how the pronunciation of O in PRO changes in words like *prospect* to a closed/short vowel sound. Students with dyslexia may continue to need these words and definitions read aloud to them as they play the matching game. That's okay. Exposure to the concepts helps build vocabulary and connects to the introductory material that comes before the decodable poems. (Note: *sodden* comes from an old word meaning the past particle of seethe or boil. It is currently used as an adjective.)

Morpho Mania #7-9 – Structured Word Inquiry: Students use a matrix to create a list of word sums for three different base elements *rest, help, spect*. Then they use words from each list to complete sentences. Each Word Matrix was created with the Mini-Matrix Maker, at www.neilramsden.co.uk/spelling/matrix. Information about the Word Matrix below is also from that website.

About the Word Matrix

1. A **Word Matrix** helps us explore word structure by organizing elements like **prefixes**, **base elements**, and **suffixes** into columns.

2. **Prefixes** are in the left column. **Base elements** are in the middle column. **Suffixes** are in the right columns.

113

Continued (page 4)

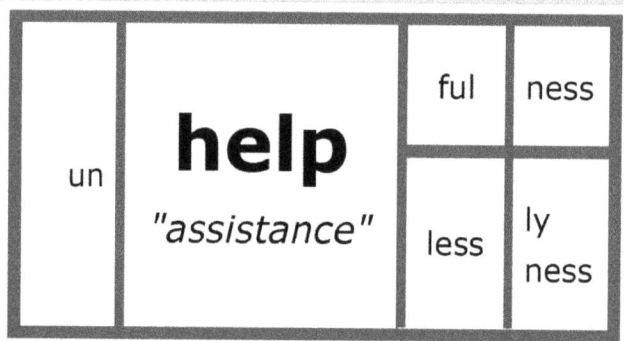

3. A **Word Sum** is created by using one element from one column at a time to construct a word. You do not have to use an element from every column, but do not skip over columns.

4. You will need the **Word Sums** to **Complete the Sentences** for activities 7-9.

Morpho Mania #10 - Etymology of Prometheus, Epimetheus, & Pandora – Study the origin of these names and the meanings of the prefixes and roots.

References:

Bowers, P. (2009). *Teaching how the written word works: Using morphological problem-solving to develop students' language skills & engagement with the written word.* Ontario, Canada: Peter Bowers

Eggleston, R. L., Marks, R. A., Sun, X., Yu, L., Zhang, K., Nickerson, N., Hu, X., Caruso, V., & Kovelman, I. (2024). Lexical morphology as a source of risk and resilience for learning to read with dyslexia: An fNIRS investigation. *Journal of Speech, Language, and Hearing Research.* https://doi.org/23814764000300140072

Farrell, L.M., & Cushen-Whte, N. (2018). Structured literacy instruction. In J.R. Birsh & S. Carreker (Eds.) *Multisensory teaching of basic language skills* (4th ed., pp. 35-72). Baltimore, MD: Paul H. Brookes Publishing Co.

Moats, L.C. (2020). Speech to print: Language Essentials for Teachers. Baltimore, MD: Paul H. Brookes Publishing Co.

Ramsden, Neil. Mini Matrix Maker at www.neilramsden.co.uk/spelling/matrix

Morpho Mania #1
Compound Words

Directions: Draw lines to combine the words from columns 1 and 2 to create compound words. Then match them to the definitions below.

1	2
bed	box
hand	bug
sand	fin
man	bell
red	hunt

1. Insects that bite people in bed - _____

2. A box filled with sand that kids play in -_____

3. A search for a criminal - _____

4. A fish with red fins - _____

5. A musical instrument - _____

ANSWERS

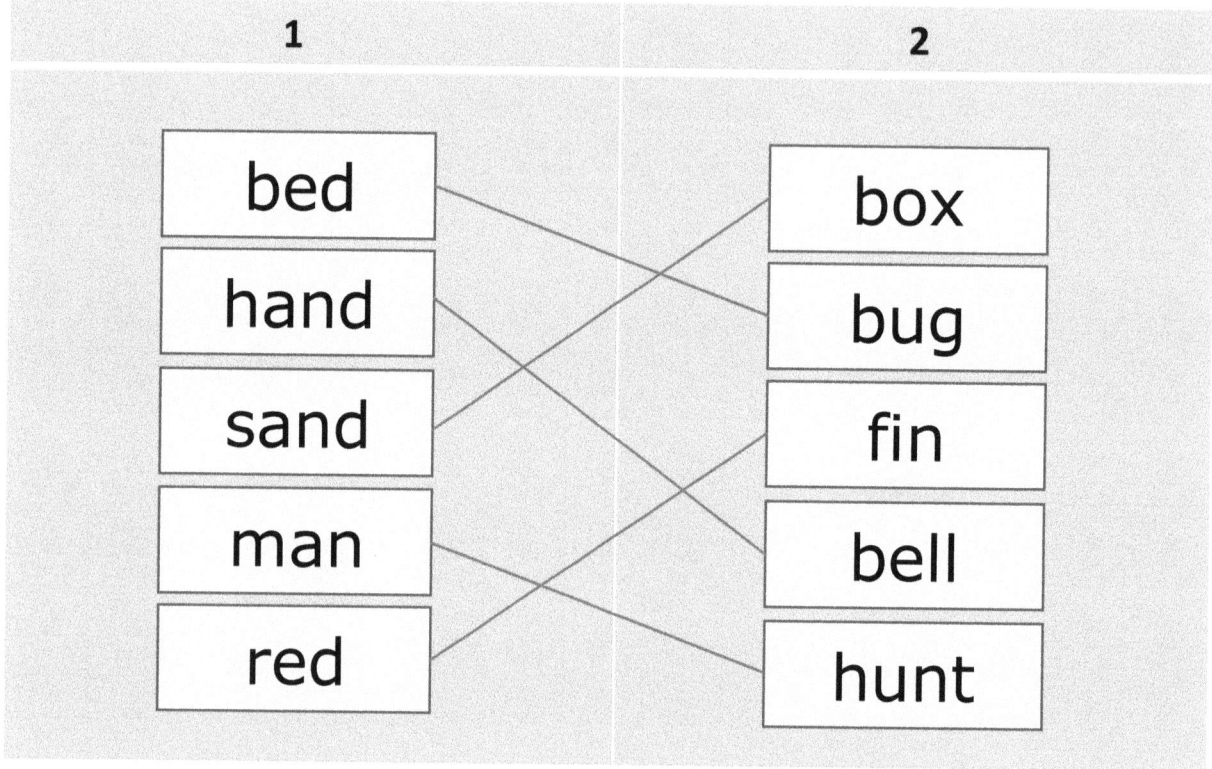

1. An insect that bites people in bed - **bedbug**

2. A box for kids filled with sand - **sandbox**

3. A search for a criminal - **manhunt**

4. A fish with fins that are red- **redfin**

5. A musical instrument - **handbell**

Morpho Mania #2
Suffix -*s*
based on *Gods and Gifts*
by Carolee Dean

Suffix -s can mean possessive, plural, or action. Read the sentences and look at the underlined word. Circle the term that describes how suffix –s is being used in that word.

Sentences	Suffix –s Use		
Ex. Jan's dog is a pug.	plural	(possessive)	action
1. Jed bent his legs.	plural	possessive	action
2. Zac camps at the picnic spot.	plural	possessive	action
3. Bob left bits of slop in the cup.	plural	possessive	action
4. The box has bands of brass.	plural	possessive	action
5. Peg grins at Sam.	plural	possessive	action
6. Don's cat is ill.	plural	possessive	action
7. Tim plans to swim.	plural	possessive	action
8. Tom's hat is big.	plural	possessive	action
9. Did Jon snap the twigs?	plural	possessive	action
10. Tim set the pits in the pan.	plural	possessive	action

ANSWERS

Sentences	Suffix -s Use		
Ex. <u>Jan's</u> dog is a pug.	plural	(possessive)	action
1. Jed bent his <u>legs</u>.	(plural)	possessive	action
2. Zac <u>camps</u> at the picnic spot.	plural	possessive	(action)
3. Bob left <u>bits</u> of slop in the cup.	(plural)	possessive	action
4. The box has <u>bands</u> of brass.	(plural)	possessive	action
5. Peg <u>grins</u> at Sam.	plural	possessive	(action)
6. <u>Don's</u> cat is ill.	plural	(possessive)	action
7. Tim <u>plans</u> to swim.	plural	possessive	(action)
8. <u>Tom's</u> hat is big.	plural	(possessive)	action
9. Did Jon snap the <u>twigs?</u>	(plural)	possessive	action
10. Tim set the <u>pits</u> in the pan.	(plural)	possessive	action

Morpho Mania #3
Suffix *-s*
based on *Gods and Gifts*
by Carolee Dean

Suffix -s can sound like /s/ or /z/. Cut out the words at the bottom and place them in the correct category. Use the word cards from the front of the book for more options.

/s/	/z/

lips	dogs	cats	plans
pits	stems	drills	lamps
rests	legs	dens	bits

ANSWERS

/s/	/z/
lips	dogs
pits	stems
rests	legs
cats	drills
lamps	dens
bits	plans

Morpho Mania #4
Suffix – *ful, ness, less*
based on *The Bandit & The Box*
by Carolee Dean

Directions: Study the words and their meanings. Then make cards for the Morpho Mania Memory Game.

ful means "full of"
ness means "state, condition, quality"
less means "without"

Word	Meaning
helpful	useful; full of help Ex: A shovel is <u>helpful</u> for digging holes.
blissful	happy; full of bliss Ex. Our trip to the park was <u>blissful</u>.
fretful	cranky; full of or causing worry. Ex. He was in a <u>fretful</u> mood.
illness	sickness; an ill condition Ex. He missed school because of an <u>illness</u>.
rapidness	speed; a rapid state Ex. She moved with <u>rapidness</u>.
witless	foolish; lacking wit Ex. The <u>witless</u> boy spent his lunch money on candy.
restless	anxious; without rest Ex. The <u>restless</u> man paced around the room all night.
restlessness	anxiety; The state of being without rest Ex. Because of his <u>restlessness</u>, he never sat still.

Memory Game Cards – Cut out the terms, paste onto game cards, turn upside down, and shuffle to play the memory game. Each player turns over two cards at a time to match the words to their meanings.

helpful	causing worry
blissful	speed
fretful	sickness
illness	foolish
rapidness	anxious
witless	happy
restless	useful

Morpho Mania #5
Suffix -en
based on *The Bandit*
by Carolee Dean

-en is a Latin suffix that has several functions including:
1) Changing a noun to an adjective – *silk to silken*
2) Changing an adjective to a verb – *glad to gladden*
3) Signifying that an action has been completed (*The grass was trodden*)
4) Changing a verb into an adjective – *forbid* to *forbidden*

Directions: Study the words and their meanings. Then make cards for the Morpho Mania Memory Game.

Word	Meaning
trodden	Trampled or crushed by walking. Ex: The grass was <u>trodden</u> under their feet.
sodden	Soggy or soaked with liquid. Ex. There was mud on the <u>sodden</u> path.
hidden	Concealed or covered. Ex. The cash was <u>hidden</u> in a box.
silken	Like silk or made of silk. Ex. The pants were made with <u>silken</u> fabric.
forbidden	Not allowed. Ex. That food is <u>forbidden</u> on my diet.

Morpho Mania #5
Memory Game
Suffix -en

Memory Game Cards – Cut out the terms, paste onto game cards, turn upside down, and shuffle to play the memory game. Each player turns over two cards at a time to match the words to their meanings.

trodden	Not allowed.
sodden	Like silk or made of silk.
silken	Soggy or soaked with liquid.
hidden	Trampled or crushed by walking.
forbidden	Concealed or covered.

Morpho Mania #6
based on *No Gift for Man*
by Carolee Dean

Pro – Latin Prefix: **before, forward, for, forth, first**

Study how the prefix PRO is used in the words below. Then print the matching game on the next page.

Word	Meaning
profess	to speak **forth** or declare -(verb) I will *profess* my love for him.
pro and con	**for** and against -(noun) He made a list of *pros and cons*.
propel	to push or move **forward** -(verb) Kick your legs to *propel* yourself through the water.
propellant	A fuel that pushes something **forward** -(noun) Which *propellant* should we use for the rocket?
product	something produced or brought **forth** -(noun) They are selling a new *product*.
protect	to shield from danger **before** something happens -(verb) The umbrella will *protect* us from the rain.
progress	movement in a **forward** direction -(noun) He is making *progress* on his report.
prospect	to look **forward** - (noun) He was looking forward to the *prospect* of buying a house. - (verb) Many people went west to *prospect* for gold.

Morpho Mania #6
Memory Game
based on *No Gift for Man*
by Carolee Dean

Memory Game Cards – Cut out the cards, paste onto construction paper, turn upside down, and shuffle to play the memory game. Each player turns over two cards at a time to match the words to their meanings.

profess	protect	a fuel that pushes something **forward**
pro and con	prospect	something produced or brought **forth**
propel	progress	to shield from danger **before** something happens
propellant	for and against	movement in a **forward** direction
product	to push or move **forward**	to look **forward**
	To speak **forth** or declare	

Directions: Use the matrix below to create as many word sums as possible. The first one is done for you.

un	**rest**	ful	ness
	"relax"	less	

Created with *Mini Matrix-Maker*, at www.neilramsden.co.uk/spelling/matrix

1._____un + rest → unrest_____
2._____
3._____
4._____
5._____

Morpho Mania #7
Structured Word Inquiry
Sentences

Directions: Use the word sums you created on the previous page to complete the sentences below.

1. I had a quiet and _____+_____ night of sleep.

2. He was _____+_____ and excited as he waited for the party to start.

3. She had a feeling of _____+_____+_____ as she anxiously counted the days until summer vacation would start.

4. The war caused extreme _____+_____.

Morpho Mania #8
Structured Word Inquiry
Word Sums

Directions: Use the matrix below to complete as many word sums as possible.

| un | **help** *"assistance"* | ful | ness |
| | | less | ly ness |

Created with *Mini Matrix-Maker*, at www.neilramsden.co.uk/spelling/matrix

1. _____
2. _____
3. _____
4. _____
5. _____
6. _____
7. _____

Directions: Use the word sums you created on the previous page to complete the sentences below.

1. The librarian was _____ + _____ to me when I was looking for a book about cars.

2. Bob has had a feeling of _____ + _____ + _____ ever since he broke his legs.

3. She was impressed by the _____ + _____ + _____ of the kids who found her lost dog.

4. The man stood by _____ + _____ + _____ as his house was destroyed by the storm.

5. If you want it to stop raining, it is _____ + _____ + _____ to yell at the clouds.

Morpho Mania #9
Structured Word Inquiry

Directions: Use the word sums to complete the sentences below. Use the back of the page if needed.

	in intro per pro	**spect** *"to see, look, observe"*	able ing ion ive or s
dis	re		ful ness

Created with *Mini Matrix-Maker*, at www.neilramsden.co.uk/spelling/matrix

1._____

2._____

3._____

4._____

5._____

6._____

7._____

8._____

Morpho Mania #9
Structured Word Inquiry
Word Sums

Directions: Use the word sums you created on the previous page to complete the sentences below.

1. The gods thought Prometheus was
   _____+_____+_____+_____
   when he stole their fire.

2. From his _____+_____+_____ on the
   cliff, Prometheus could see what was happening
   below.

3. He had a lot of time for thinking and
   _____+_____+_____.

4. They had big plans and
   _____+_____+____ for the future.

5. Pandora wanted to _____+_____
   the contents of the box.

ANSWERS

Morpho Mania #7 – Rest
1. restful
2. restless
3. restlessness
4. unrest

Morpho Mania #8 - Help
1. helpful
2. helpless
3. helpfulness
4. helplessly
5. unhelpful

Morpho Mania #9 - Spect
1. disrespectful
2. perspective
3. introspection
4. prospects
5. inspect

Morph Mania #10
Etymology
Prometheus, Epimetheus
& Pandora

based on *Gods and Gifts* by Carolee Dean

Prometheus was a Titan whose name meant "forthinker" or "forethought. *Pro* (before) + *methos* related to *mathein* "to learn." from the PIE root *men* "to think."

Pro is a Greek prefix meaning "before, forward, for, forth, first" Other *pro* words include *protect, propel*

Epimetheus was the brother of Prometheus. His name meant "afterthought." He didn't think about things until he'd already messed them up.

Epi is a Greek prefix meaning "upon, over, after, near." Other epi words include *epidemic, epidermis*

Pandora was the woman created by the gods as a gift and a bride for Epimetheus. *Pan* "all" + *doron* "gift" from the PIE *do* "to give." Her name could mean *all-gifted* since the gods gave her many gifts, or it could mean *giver of all* since she is the one who opened the forbidden box which unleashed many bad "gifts."

Pan is a Greek prefix meaning "all, every" Other *pan* words include *pandemic, panorama*

Directions: Find at least one more word to go with each prefix below:

Pro _____

Epi _____

Pan _____

VOCABULARY

INTRODUCTION

Vocabulary is a foundational building block of both listening and reading comprehension, but it can be challenging to include robust vocabulary when focusing on limited constructs such as closed syllable types. On the other hand, even these most basic word forms can provide opportunities for exploring advanced vocabulary, especially when multi-syllable words are included. When vocabulary is content-rich and comes from material related to the curriculum, repeated exposure to words is more natural. Read about vocabulary on the page for COR Instruction on the website.

The stories in Level 1 of the HOT ROD series have words divided into syllables. However, the vocabulary lists do NOT divide words. Have students place a / between syllables if needed.

Pre-teach new words before students are asked to read them in context. It can also be helpful to teach students strategies for determining the meaning of new words on their own by looking at the context **before** they are told the definition. Students with dyslexia need even more exposure to a word than their peers, so if they have already been introduced to a word, it is still helpful to explore the word in context. Context is especially important for understanding multiple-meaning words.

Rereading helps students develop confidence and fluency, but there needs to be a meaningful reason for rereading a text. Ask students to reread the story to find multi-meaning words and to decide which meaning of the word applies to the story.

References:
Wright, T.S., & Neuman, S.B. (2015). The power of content-rich vocabulary instruction. *Perspectives on Language and Literacy*, 41 (3), 25-28.

Shanahan, T. (2015). Are you lactating? On the importance of academic language. *Perspectives on Language and Literacy, 41*(3), 14-16.

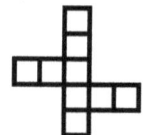

ACTIVITIES

Word Clues – Seek and Find: Sometimes the meaning of a new word is stated directly within the context of a nearby sentence. In this activity, students underline the definition that is provided in the context.

Multiple Meaning Match Up – Students match words in a memory game as they explore double meanings.

WOW (Wonder of Words) Vocabulary: The vocabulary word lists may be used for a variety of games listed below. One-syllable words. Even short words may be unfamiliar to some students and will present an opportunity to learn new word meanings. Students with dyslexia may need some of the definitions read aloud to them. Instruct students to divide the words if needed. Some words are from the story poems, some are from the introduction or background sections. Some are from the non-fiction article "Bats and Their Amazing Skills." A blank Vocabulary Template and blank Vocabulary Foldable have been provided for students who are ready to tackle the additional words and definitions not listed here from the Background Information section of *Gods and Gifts* which may be found in the chapter book.

Games & Activities for WOW

1. **Alphabet** – Cut out the words and put them in alphabetical order.

2. **Vocabulary Foldable** – Follow the directions to complete a vocabulary foldable.

3. **Memory Game** – Make two copies of the words. Glue them onto construction paper and play the Memory Game by turning the cards face down. Pick two at a time, looking for a match. Read the words out loud as you turn them over and give the meaning. Start with 5 sets of words. When that is manageable, go up to 6, then 7, then 8 or more.

4. **Go Fish** –Make two sets of cards and play Go Fish.

5. **Boom Cards** - Additional Games may be found at Boom Learning

Word Clues
Seek and Find
based on *Gods and Gifts*
by Carolee Dean

DIRECTIONS: Read the word in the left column. Find it in the sentence and circle it. Then underline the information that helps you understand the meaning of the word.

Word	Meaning
asp	He went to the hospital after he was bitten by an asp, a very poisonous snake.
kestrel	A kestrel is smaller than other types of falcons.
basset	They needed a hunting dog, so they bought a basset.
spit	He put the chunks of beef on a spit, a rod for cooking meat.
dusk	Moths come out at dusk, the time between day and night.
distant	They came from a distant land that was quite far away.
class	She was trendy and stylish and always dressed with class.
scan	When you scan a page, you don't read every word, you just glance over it quickly.
mumps	We have vaccines for diseases like mumps.
brass	The bells were made of brass, a shiny yellow metal.

Word Clues
based on *Gods and Gifts*
by Carolee Dean

ANSWERS

Word	Meaning
asp	He went to the hospital after he was bitten by an (asp,) a very *poisonous* <u>snake.</u>
kestrel	A (kestrel) is <u>smaller</u> than other <u>types</u> <u>of</u> <u>falcons</u>.
basset	They need<u>ed a hunting dog,</u> so they bought a (basset.)
spit	He put the chunks of beef on a (spit,) <u>a</u> <u>rod for cooking meat.</u>
dusk	Moths come out at (dusk,) <u>the time</u> <u>between day and night.</u>
distant	They came from a (distant) land that was quite <u>far away.</u>
class	She was <u>trendy and stylish</u> and always dressed with (class.)
scan	When you (scan) a page, you don't read every word, you just <u>glance over it</u> <u>quickly.</u>
mumps	<u>We have</u> vaccines for <u>diseases</u> like (mumps.)
brass	The bells were made of (brass,) <u>a shiny</u> <u>yellow metal.</u>

Multiple Meaning Match Up #1
based on *No Gift for Man*
by Carolee Dean

Directions: 1. Make two copies of the words below.
2 Cut out the words and glue them onto construction paper.
3. Play the Memory Matching game.
4. Make sure you choose words with the same meanings.

bat a wooden club	**bat** a flying mammal
drill a type of monkey	**drill** a thing that makes holes
hog a swine	**hog** a selfish person
rat a type of rodent	**rat** to tattle

Multiple Meaning Match Up #2
based on *The Bandit*
by Carolee Dean

Directions: 1. Make two copies of the words below.
2 Cut out the words and glue them onto construction paper.
3. Play the Memory Matching game.
4. Make sure you choose words with the same meanings.

pelt to hit repeatedly	**pelt** animal skin
land to bring to the ground	**land** the ground
last at the end	**last** to continue
spit A rod	**spit** eject saliva
bluff a cliff	**bluff** to fool or trick

Multiple Meaning Match Up #3
based on *Gods and Gifts*
by Carolee Dean

Directions: 1. Make two copies of the words below.
2 Cut out the words and glue them onto construction paper.
3. Play the Memory Matching game.
4. Make sure you choose words with the same meanings.

top highest point	**top** a twirling toy	**band** a musical group
spin to turn	**spin** to make thread or yarn	**band** a strip of material
class a group of students	**class** style	**jam** blockage or obstruction
craft to make	**craft** a hobby or skill	**jam** like jelly with chunks of fruit

WOW Vocabulary #1
based on *No Gift for Man*
by Carolee Dean

1. Study the words below.
2. Use them to make a vocabulary foldable.

Word	Meaning
asp	a poisonous snake
basset	a breed of hound dog
drill	a type of baboon
falcon	a large bird of prey
jackal	a wild dog
kestrel	a small falcon
linnet	a small songbird
siskin	a small yellow bird

WOW Vocabulary #2
based on *The Bandit*
by Carolee Dean

1. Study the words below.
2. Use them to make a vocabulary foldable.

Word	Meaning
bliss	happiness
bluff	a cliff
bog	wet and mushy soil with dead plants in it
cliff	a steep rock face
craft	to make with skill
crag	the rough part of a rock
crept	to creep (past tense)
dusk	between day and night
fled	to flee or leave (past tense)
glen	a small valley

WOW Vocabulary #3
based on *The Bandit*
by Carolee Dean

1. Study the words below.
2. Use them to make a vocabulary foldable.

Word	Meaning
nab	to catch
pelt	to hit repeatedly
rant	to talk in a wild or angry way
smelt	to melt metal to separate it
sped	to speed (past tense)
spit	a sharp rod for cooking meat
strand	A fiber or thread
swift	fast
trod	to tread or trample (past tense)
vast	very large

WOW Vocabulary #4
based on *The Bandit*
by Carolee Dean

1. Study the 2-syllable words below.
2. Use them to make a vocabulary foldable.

Word	Meaning
anvil	an iron block used for bending metal into a desired shape.
bandit	a robber
blissful	full of happiness
canyon	a valley with steep sides
common	simple
crimson	deep red
dismal	sad or gloomy
distant	far
fennel	a plant related to parsley
frantic	wild with fear

WOW Vocabulary #5
based on *The Bandit*
by Carolee Dean

1. Study the 2-syllable words below.
2. Use them to make a vocabulary foldable.

Word	Meaning
funnel	something shaped like a cone
gallant	brave, noble, and polite
grandest	the most grand or impressive
helpful	giving aid or help
kindred	like family
prospects	things to look forward to
pummel	to beat with fists
rascal	a bum or dishonest person
rustic	rural or from the back-country
wistful	wishful

WOW Vocabulary #6
based on *The Box*
by Carolee Dean

1. Study the words below.
2. Use them to make a vocabulary foldable.

Word	Meaning
combat	a fight
crimson	a deep red color
indignant	angry
mumps	a type of virus
rend	to tear
scandal	a disgraceful action
splendid	excellent
strep	a bacterial infection
tempest	a windy storm
vespid	a type of wasp
yen	a desire

WOW Vocabulary #7
based on "Bats and Their Amazing Skills"
by Carolee Dean

Explore the Wonder of Words with terms from "Bats and Their Amazing Skills" found in this Activity Book.

1. Study the list below.
2. Use them to make a vocabulary foldable.

Word	Meaning
Aves	birds
Chiroptera	"hand wing" in Greek
echolocation	the ability to locate objects through sound that bounces back
launch	to thrust forward, outward, or upward
Mammalia	mammals
radar	a device for determining the location of an object
roost	to settle down for rest or sleep
vertebrate	an animal with a spine

WOW Vocabulary #8
based on the Introduction and
Background Sections
of *Gods and Gifts*
by Carolee Dean

Explore the Wonder of Words with terms from Introduction Background Sections of *Gods and Gifts*.

1. Study the list below.
2. Use them to make a vocabulary foldable.

Word	Meaning
carbon	element found in organic matter
dross	scum or dregs
hieroglyphic	written with pictures or symbols
indigenous	native
pictograph	prehistoric wall painting
prehensile	able to grasp things
revenge	repayment for a wrong
translated	rewritten in another language

WOW Vocabulary Template
Blank
by Carolee Dean

1. Find words from the Background Section of *Gods and Gifts* and write them in the left column.
2. Write the MEANING in the right column.
3. Use the words to make a vocabulary foldable.

Word	Meaning

Vocabulary Foldable
Example

Directions:

1. Write (or cut and paste) 8 words from the WOW Vocabulary List on a blank vocabulary foldable.

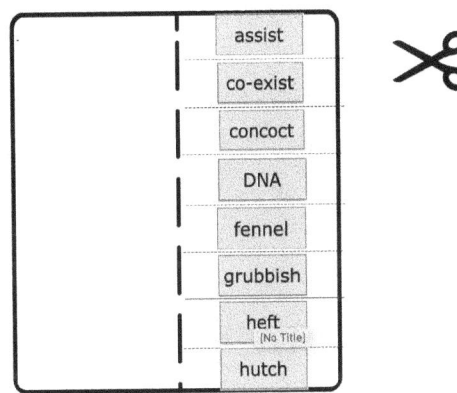

2. Then cut on the dotted lines between the words.

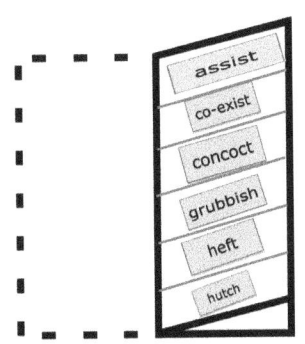

3. Fold the paper in half lengthwise.

4. Open the foldable and write the definitions for the words on the inside on the right. Draw pictures to go with the word on the left.

5. Close the foldable. Test yourself by reading a word out loud. Say the definition. Then open the foldable and see if you were right.

6. When you are done studying the words and definitions cut them apart, glue them onto construction paper, and play a memory matching game.

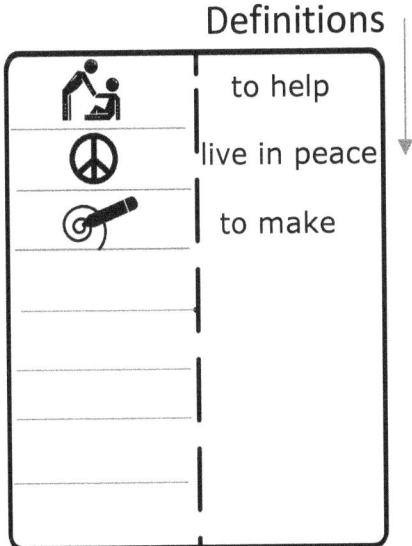

Vocabulary Foldable
based on *Gods and Gifts*
by Carolee Dean

SENTENCE CONSTRUCTION

Many students, even those without reading challenges, have difficulty determining if a sentence is complete or incomplete. Part of the reason is that most kids are taught that a sentence must have a noun and a verb. Unfortunately, confusion arises with words that can be both nouns and verbs such as jet: *He flew on a jet. I will jet to the store.*

Before starting the activities, talk with students about the meaning of the terms *Subject* and *Predicate*. See examples and additional information at COR Instruction page on the website. Explain how poetry is not always written in complete sentences even when there is a period at the end of a line. Also, a capitalized word does not always indicate the start of a new sentence.

Sentence Mania Activity: Students explore multiple-meaning words from the vocabulary section that sometimes function as nouns, sometimes as verbs, and sometimes as adjectives. They will use the context of the sentence to help them decide how the word is being used. If students need additional support, instruct them to identify the verb in each sentence by placing a box around it. The activity incorporates 27 words with /s/ or /z/ sounds and is useful for SLPs to use for articulation practice at the sentence level. It is also available in a Boom Card Format for an additional fee at https://wow.boomlearning.com Go to the Store for Word Travel Press and look up Parts of Speech: Noun, Verb, or Adjective?

Sentence Construction #1-2: Sentence Combining. Sentence combining improves both reading and writing skills. Decodable books often contain short sentences, so it is important to provide experiences with longer sentences. Use the conjunctions provided to create longer sentences. Demonstrate how to use a comma if the information that comes after it could stand alone as a sentence. *The pig can grunt, and the pig can dig.* **versus** *The pig can grunt and dig.*

Sentence Construction #3: Who is Doing What? Ask questions about an illustration from the book to create one long sentence.

Sentence Construction #4: Identifying Complete Sentences. Determine if sentences are complete or incomplete. Then decide what is missing.

References:
Hochman, J.C. & MacDermott-Duffy, B. (2018). Composition: Evidence-based instruction. In J.R. Birsh & S. Carreker (Eds.) Multisensory teaching of basic language skills (4th ed., pp. 205-253. Baltimore, MD: Paul H. Brookes Publishing Co.

Nelson, N.W. (2013). Syntax development in the school-age years: implications for assessment and intervention. *Perspectives on Language and Literacy*. 39 (3), 9-15.

Van Cleave, W. (2014). *Writing matters: Developing sentence skills in students of all ages (Second Edition)*. Greenville, SC: W.V.C.ED

Sentence Mania
Noun * Verb * Adjective
based on *The Bandit*
by Carolee Dean

Directions: The underlined words below have more than one meaning. Sometimes they act like verbs (an action), sometimes they act like nouns (a person, place, or thing), and sometimes they act like adjectives to describe a noun. Circle VERB, NOUN, or ADJECTIVE based on how the word is used in the sentence. Ask yourself if it is an action, a thing, or a description.

EXAMPLES:
1. Did Bill <u>craft</u> that box out of wood? (Verb) Noun Adjective
2. Bill sells his <u>crafts</u> at the fair. Verb (Noun) Adjective
3. Bill attends <u>craft</u> fairs to sell his boxes. Verb Noun (Adjective)

HINT: In the first sentence, Bill's ACTION is to craft a box out of wood. In the second sentence, he is selling the THING he has made. The third sentence DESCRIBES the type of fairs Bill attends.

Word	Part of Speech		
	ACTION	THING	DESCRIPTION
1. Stan was in a hip hop <u>band.</u>	Verb	Noun	Adjective
2. Sid went on a <u>band</u> trip	Verb	Noun	Adjective
3. Sam sat on the sodden <u>land</u>.	Verb	Noun	Adjective
4. Insects <u>land</u> in grass and on plants.	Verb	Noun	Adjective
5. Will the milk <u>last</u> or will it rot?	Verb	Noun	Adjective
6. Sis got the <u>last</u> gift.	Verb	Noun	Adjective
7. Did the sullen man just <u>spit</u> in the pond?	Verb	Noun	Adjective
8. Sal will grill the chicken on a <u>spit</u>.	Verb	Noun	Adjective
9. The sultan sat at the top of the <u>bluff</u>.	Verb	Noun	Adjective
10. Scot <u>bluffs</u> a lot and kids his pals.	Verb	Noun	Adjective
11. The <u>pelt</u> was with the jackets.	Verb	Noun	Adjective
12. Did Vulcan <u>pelt</u> the rascal with his fist?	Verb	Noun	Adjective

Sentence Mania
Noun * Verb * Adjective
based on *The Bandit*
by Carolee Dean

ANSWERS

Word	Part of Speech		
	ACTION	THING	DESCRIPTION
1. Stan was in a hip hop <u>band</u>.	Verb	(Noun)	Adjective
2. Sid went on a <u>band</u> trip	Verb	Noun	(Adjective)
3. Sam sat on the sodden <u>land</u>.	Verb	(Noun)	Adjective
4. Insects <u>land</u> in grass and on plants.	(Verb)	Noun	Adjective
5. Will the milk <u>last</u> or will it rot?	(Verb)	Noun	Adjective
6. Sis got the <u>last</u> gift.	Verb	Noun	(Adjective)
7. Did the sullen man just <u>spit</u> in the pond?	(Verb)	Noun	Adjective
8. Sal will grill the chicken on a <u>spit</u>.	Verb	(Noun)	Adjective
9. The sultan sat at the top of the <u>bluff</u>.	Verb	(Noun)	Adjective
10. Scot <u>bluffs</u> a lot and kids his pals.	(Verb)	Noun	Adjective
11. The <u>pelt</u> was with the jackets.	Verb	(Noun)	Adjective
12. Did Vulcan <u>pelt</u> the rascal with his fist?	(Verb)	Noun	Adjective

Sentence Construction #1
Sentence Combining
based on *No Gift for Man*
by Carolee Dean

Directions:

Use the conjunction in **bold** to combine the 2 short sentences.

Example:

(and) The dog can run. The dog can bark.

The dog can run, and it can bark. OR

The dog can run and bark.

(for) The man is sad. The man did not get a gift.

(and) The pig can grunt. The pig can dig.

(nor) The man did not get a fin. The man did not get a web.

(but) The crab got a shell. The man did not get a gift.

(or) It can get a fin. It can get a web.

(yet) A bat is not a bird. A bat can fly.

(so) The pig did not get wings. The pig can not fly.

Sentence Construction #1
Sentence Combining
based on *No Gift for Man*
by Carolee Dean

ANSWERS

(for) The man is sad. The man did not get a gift.

The man is sad, for the man did not get a gift.

(and) The pig can grunt. The pig can dig.

The pig can grunt, and it can dig.   OR
The pig can grunt and dig.

(nor) The man did not get a fin. The man did not get a web.

The man did not get a fin, nor did he get a web.

(but) The crab got a shell. The man did not get a gift.

The crab got a shell, but the man did not get a gift.

(or) It can get a fin. It can get a web.

It can get a fin, or it can get a web.   OR
It can get a fin or a web.

(yet) A bat is not a bird. A bat can fly.

A bat is not a bird, yet it can fly.

(so) The pig did not get wings. The pig can not fly.

The pig did not get wings, so it can not fly.

Sentence Construction #2
Sentence Combining
based on *The Bandit*
by Carolee Dean

Directions:
Use the conjunction in **bold** to combine the 2 short sentences.

Example:
(and) The dog can run. The dog can bark.
The dog can run, and it can bark.   OR
The dog can run and bark.

(for) The Titan stole fire. The Titan wanted a gift for humans.

(and) People could cook food. People could melt metal.

(nor) Men did not get wings for flying. Men did not get night vision.

(but) The Titan was punished. Humans got to keep fire.

(or) Men could live in caves. Men could build houses.

(yet) The Titan was a god. The Titan defied the king of the gods.

(so) The Titan stole fire. Zeus had him chained to a cliff.

Sentence Construction #2
Sentence Combining
based on *The Bandit*
by Carolee Dean

ANSWERS

(for) The Titan stole fire. The Titan wanted a gift for humans.

The Titan stole fire, for he wanted a gift for humans.

(and) People could cook food. People could melt metal.
People could cook food, and they could melt metal.
People could cook food and melt metal.

(nor) Men did not get wings for flying. Men did not get night vision.
Men did not get wings for flying, nor did they get night vision.
Men did not get wings nor night vision.

(but) The Titan was punished. Humans got to keep fire.

The Titan was punished, but humans got to keep fire.

(or) Men could live in caves. Men could build houses.

Men could live in caves, or they could build houses.
Men could live in caves or build houses.

(yet) The Titan was a god. The Titan defied the king of the gods.

The Titan was a god, yet he defied the king of the gods.

(so) The Titan stole from the gods. Zeus had him chained to a cliff.

The Titan stole from the gods, so Zeus had him chained to a cliff.

Sentence Construction #3
Who is Doing What?
based on *Gods and Gifts*
by Carolee Dean

Directions:
1. Pick an illustration from the book.
2. Describe what is going on in the illustration by answering the questions below.
3. Use your answers to construct one long sentence.

Question	Response
1. What is the name of an animal or character in the illustration?	
2. What are they doing?	
3. How? (ex. quickly, slowly, backward, with care).	
4. Where is this happening?	
5. Why might they be doing this action? This may not be in the picture. Use your imagination.	

Use the information above to create one long sentence:

_____

_____

_____

Sentence Construction #4
Identifying Complete Sentences
based on *No Gift for Man*
by Carolee Dean

A complete sentence requires two things: a SUBJECT (Who or What is doing)
+ a PREDICATE (What they are doing)

Directions:
1. Read each line below. Is it a complete sentence? Circle YES or NO.
2. If NO - circle SUBJECT or PREDICATE (Verb) to show what is missing.

Line of Verse	Complete Sentence		What's Missing?	
1. Kes·trel, fal·con.	yes	no	subject	predicate
2. The fox can hunt.	yes	no	subject	predicate
3. A gift for the rat.	yes	no	subject	predicate
4. Ran fast.	yes	no	subject	predicate
5. The bat can drop.	yes	no	subject	predicate
6. One got silk.	yes	no	subject	predicate
7. The pug can smell.	yes	no	subject	predicate
8. The bass got a fin.	yes	no	subject	predicate
9. Can hunt.	yes	no	subject	predicate
10. Jac·kal, lin·net.	yes	no	subject	predicate

Sentence Construction #4
Identifying Complete Sentences
based on *No Gift for Man*
by Carolee Dean

ANSWERS

Line of Verse	Complete Sentence		What's Missing?	
1. Kes·trel, fal·con.	yes	(no)	subject	(predicate)
2. The fox can hunt	(yes)	no	subject	predicate
3. A gift for the rat.	yes	(no)	subject	(predicate)
4. Ran fast.	yes	(no)	(subject)	predicate
5. The bat can drop.	(yes)	no	subject	predicate
6. One got silk.	(yes)	no	subject	predicate
7. The pug can smell.	(yes)	no	subject	predicate
8. The bass got a fin.	(yes)	no	subject	predicate
9. Can hunt.	yes	(no)	(subject)	predicate
10. Jac·kal, lin·net.	yes.	(no)	subject	(predicate)

STORY FRAMES

INTRODUCTION

The Story Analysis is based on my book, *Story Frames for Teaching Literacy: Enhancing Student Learning Through the Power of Storytelling* (Paul H. Brookes Publishing Co., 2021). That book is not needed to complete this story analysis on the next few pages, but if you would like to take a deeper dive into narrative intervention with access to 35 adaptable lesson plans along with downloadable resources, you can find my book at Brookes Publishing. The lesson plans include a more detailed approach to summary writing as well as a detailed discussion of how writing expectations change across the grade levels.

Story Plot Analysis – *The Creation of Man* Story Analysis incorporates the first three books of the Hot Rod Series (Set 1, Books 1-3) including *No Gift for Man*, *The Bandit*, and *The Box*. All three are also found in the chapter book, *Gods and Gifts*. Read all three stories, and then use the completed storyboard on the next few pages to help guide students to complete the blank storyboard.

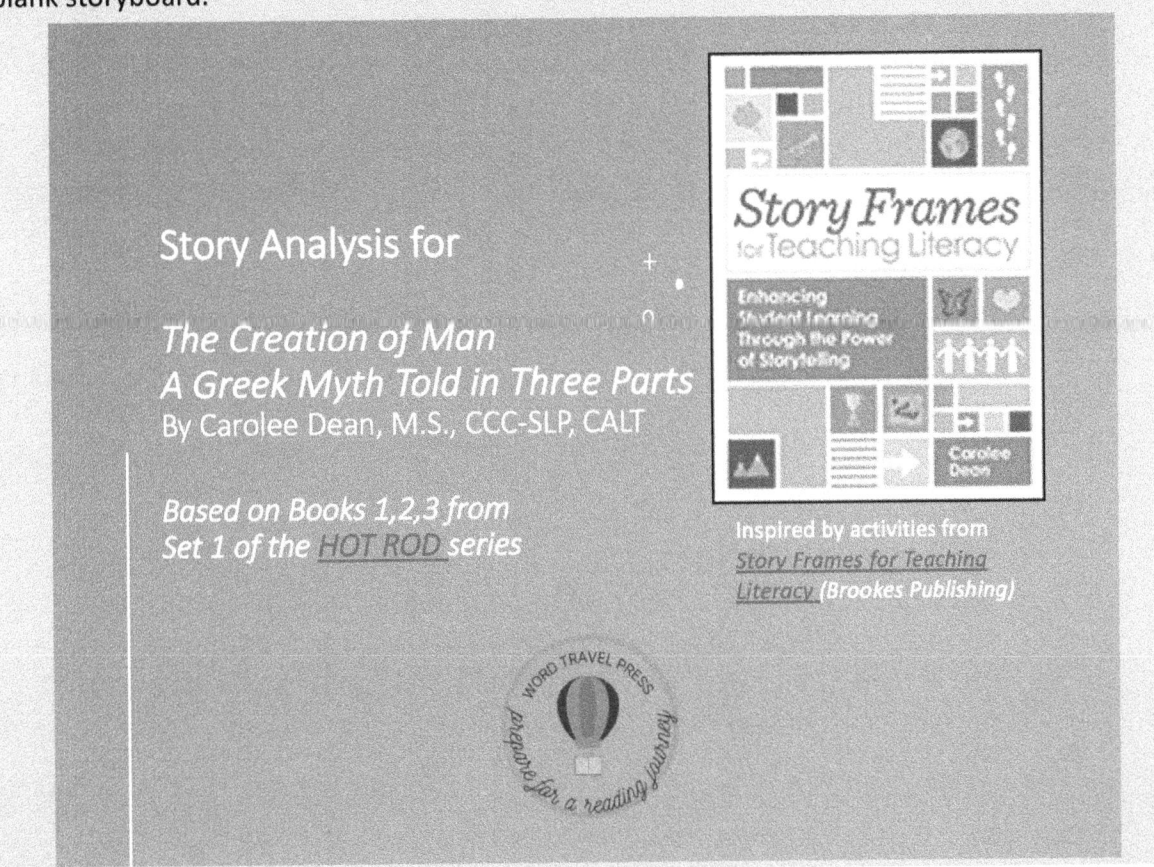

STORY FRAMES

PLOT ANALYSIS

The BASIC STORYBOARD is based upon the traditional story analysis outlined by Stein, N., & Glenn, C. (1979). An analysis of story comprehension in elementary school children. In R. Freedle (Ed.), New directions in discourse processing (Vol. 2, pp. 53-120). Norwood, NJ: Ablex.

Their story elements include *setting, initiating events, internal responses, internal plans, attempts, direct consequences*, and *reactions*. The 8 elements of the *Story Frames* BASIC STORYBOARD are below:

1. **Ordinary World**: The Main Character (MC) and setting are described.
2. **Call and Response**: An initiating event occurs to get the action going and the main character's inward and/or outward response to that event are described.
3. **Problems and Prizes:** A problem or a prize (or both) are described
4. **Plans**: The MC makes plans that may be obvious or implied.
5. **Attempt**: The MC attempts to attain the goal with consequences.
6. **Attempt**: The MC makes another attempt to attain the goal with consequences.
7. **Climax**: A final attempt to attain the goal is made.
8. **Reward**: The MC receives an award or consequence. Internal responses to the events and outcome of the story are explored.

The BASIC STORYBOARD is from *Story Frames for Teaching Literacy: Enhancing Student Learning Through the Power of Storytelling* (Brookes Publishing, 2021) by Carolee Dean

1. After reading the story poems, the student uses the blank version of the BASIC STORYBOARD and either draws stick figures, writes keywords, or both in each square to show what is happening in each frame of the story. Model as needed. This step may be completed as a class or individually. Storyboards with the content described are for teacher reference.
2. The completed student storyboard may then be used to retell the story verbally or to write a summary. Each row of the storyboard creates a paragraph except for the bottom row, which functions like a word wall and contains key terms.
3. An 8x11 printable version of each storyboard may be found in the downloadable PDFs. Find the code near the end of this Activity Book.

The longer, COMPLETE STORYBOARD version with 12 story frames is available on page 133 of *Story Frames for Teaching Literacy: Enhancing Student Learning Through the Power of Storytelling*.

STORY FRAMES

PLOT ANALYSIS

Ordinary World	Call & Response	Problem & Prize	Plan

Attempt	Attempt	Climax	Reward

Vocabulary	People & Places	Conjunctions		Transitions
forethought	Epimetheus (ĕp-ə-MĒ-thē-əs)	and	although	first
afterthought	Olympus (ō-LĬM-pəs)	but	before	eventually
create	Olympians (ō-LĬM-pē-ənz)	yet	after	next
present	Pandora (pan-DOR-ə)	or	unless	consequently
gift	Prometheus (prō-MĒ-thē-əs)	so	while	last
fragment	Titans (TĪ-tənz)	then	where	surprisingly
indignant	Vulcan (VUL-kən)	because	even if	in addition
Antagonistic	Zeus (zūs)	when		finally
Revenge				as a result
Splendid				
temptest				

STORY FRAMES

Story Frames
for Teaching Literacy

Enhancing
Student Learning
Through the Power
of Storytelling

Carolee
Dean

PLOT ANALYSIS

Story Frames (Basic Version) – THE CREATION OF MAN by Carolee Dean

Ordinary World	Call & Response	Problem & Prize	Plan
The war between the Titans and the Olympians ended and Zeus was getting a little bored.	Zeus asked Prometheus and his brother, Epimetheus, to fill the world with living creatures. They agreed to take on the task.	Epimetheus gave away all the gifts to the animals and there was nothing left for man.	Prometheus wanted something special for mankind, so he planned to steal fire from Mount Olympus.

Attempt or Event	Attempt or Event	Climax	Reward
Prometheus took a small bit of fire from Mount Olympus and hid it in a plant. He shared the gift of fire with humans. They could keep warm and heat their food.	Zeus chained Prometheus to a rock as punishment for stealing fire. Then the gods got revenge on mankind by creating Pandora and giving her to Epimetheus as a bride.	As a wedding gift, the gods gave Pandora a box and told her never to open it. When she finally did, all sorts of evil things came out like war, disease, and sickness.	The last "gift" in the box was hope. It kept mankind going in spite of the evils that came out of the box. Eventually, Heracles freed Prometheus.

Vocabulary	People & Places	Conjunctions		Transitions
forethought afterthought create present gift fragment indignant revenge splendid temptest	Epimetheus (ĕp-ə-MĒ-thē-əs) Olympus (ō-LĬM-pəs) Olympians (ō-LĬM-pē-ənz) Pandora (pan-DOR-ə) Prometheus (prō-MĒ-thē-əs) Titans (TĪ-tənz) Vulcan (VUL-kən) Zeus (zūs)	and but yet or so then because when	although before after unless while where even if	first eventually next consequently last surprisingly in addition finally as a result

COMPREHENSION

INTRODUCTION

PAGES – The PAGES strategy includes five key elements that have been shown to improve comprehension: They may be used while listening or reading. P= Pause and Picture, A= Ask Questions, G = Go Back or Go Forward, E = Explore Words, S = Summarize

What's Your Text Type? –Knowing text types helps the reader frame the information and understand the author's purpose. In this activity, students first learn about the features of the different types of text in the Text Types Guide and the signal words that go with each type. Then they read an excerpt based on *Gods and Gifts* and use the Text Type Guide to help them decide on the text type.

Comprehension Questions - Many older students are expected to answer questions using a RACE format or something similar. Struggling learners need this process broken down into manageable steps and modeled. After reading or listening to the non-fiction article included in this Activity Book entitled, "Bats and Their Amazing Skiils," students answer comprehension questions by restating the question before providing the answer. Word count and approximate grade level are provided if you would like to calculate reading fluency either before or after reading for comprehension. Headings are not included in the word count. Remember that many students with writing challenges will need the additional support of being able to answer verbally or using a voice-to-text option to create written responses. That's okay. They are still learning the grade level expectations and are growing in their ability to give more detailed answers.

RACE Responses - Students ready for complete RACE Responses may add to their responses above by citing evidence from the text and further explaining their answers. Students with learning differences may need the selection read aloud for them a second or third time.

Struggling readers often miss out on these rich writing opportunities. Even after their decoding skills improve, they may still lag behind their peers in written language development. It is important to scaffold these advanced written responses and provide adequate support so that written language goals are both challenging and attainable.

Dean, C. (2021). *Story frames for teaching literacy: Enhancing student learning through the power of storytelling*. Baltimore, MD: Paul H. Brookes Publishing Co.

Hennessy, N.L. (2021). *The reading comprehension blueprint: Helping students make meaning from text*. Baltimore, MD: Paul H. Brookes Publishing Co.

PAGES

Use this strategy when reading or listening to something read aloud.

Picture – Pause after a **period**, a **paragraph**, or a **page** of text and try to form a mental **picture** of what you have just read.

Ask – There are many questions you might **ask** yourself about what you have read, but the first and most important two are, "Was I able to form a picture?" and "Does that picture make sense?" You may also **ask** clarification questions and questions about Who is Doing What? Also, **ask** yourself if there are words that you don't know or that don't make sense.

Go Back or Go Forward – Do you need to **go back** and reread what you just read? Sometimes you need to keep moving **forward**. A confusing word or reference may become clearer in the next sentence or when you finish the sentence you are reading.

Explore words - Are there unfamiliar **words** or concepts that need to be looked up in the dictionary or in another reference?

Summarize – Once the above steps have been taken, put the information into your own words. If you are not ready to **summarize**, you may need to go back and explore some of the steps again.

Text Type Guide

Use the information below to decide on the text types in the next activity.

Type of Text	Signal Words
Description – Sensory details are used to describe a person, place, or thing.	looks like, sounds like, feels like, for example, such as, characterized by
Sequence – an order of events, timeline, or steps in a process.	before, during, after, first, second, next, then, finally
Compare and Contrast – How two or more things are alike or different.	same, as well as, similar, in common, different, although, however, on the other hand, in comparison, either/or
Problem and Solution – What is wrong and how to fix it.	because, resolved, result, so that, consequently,
Cause and Effect – How or why an event happened and the result.	because, since, as a result, caused by, led to, therefore, when/then, if/then

Dean, C. (2021). *Story frames for teaching literacy: Enhancing student learning through the power of storytelling*. Baltimore, MD: Paul H. Brookes Publishing Co.

Hennessy, N.L. (2021). *The reading comprehension blueprint: Helping students make meaning from text.* Baltimore, MD: Paul H. Brookes Publishing Co.

What's My Text Type? (1-3)

Directions: Read each paragraph below from *Gods and Gifts* by Carolee Dean. Identify which paragraph goes with which text type.

1. Some examples of Mayan writing date back to 300 to 200 BCE. While the Greeks used letters to represent the individual sounds in words, the Maya used hieroglyphic images. Similar to the Greek alphabet, some of these symbols, also called glyphs, stood for sounds. Unlike the Greek alphabet, it was usually consonant-vowel syllable combinations rather than single sounds.

2. The Maya gods went through four attempts to create early humans. First, they made the animals, but none of them could speak. They could not praise the gods. Second, they created people out of earth and mud, but these early humans kept crumbling and falling apart. For their third attempt, the gods created people out of wood.

3. The Maya painted their images on walls and pots. They carved them in stucco and monuments of stone. They even engraved them into objects found in nature such as shells, wood, jade, and bone. They created paper made from tree bark and used the tree bark to make folded books. These books contained colorful hieroglyphic images.

Test Type:	Paragraph #:
Description	_____
Sequence	_____
Compare and Contrast	_____
Problem and Solution	_____
Cause and Effect	_____

What's My Text Type? (4-6)

Directions: Read each paragraph below from *Gods and Gifts* by Carolee Dean. Identify which paragraph goes with which text type.

4. Early man ate a lot of raw vegetables, fruits, and meats. The problem with eating raw meat was that it took a lot of time and energy to chew and digest it. Also, it contained bacteria that could make people very sick. Fire killed bacteria which resulted in fewer people getting sick. Cooking meat also made it easier to chew. Consequently, cooking saved much time and effort that could be used for other activities.

5. Charcoal was made by heating wood. It had to be buried under dirt, grass, and plant material with a few air holes at the bottom and top. Burying the wood resulted in limiting the oxygen. When oxygen was limited, the wood did not catch fire. Instead, this condition caused the wood to smolder and burn very slowly. The heat got rid of any moisture. What was left behind was the black carbon chunks we call charcoal.

6. At first, early humans used wood to fuel fires. Then around 5500 to 5000 BCE they started using charcoal. With this hotter fire, humans could smelt ore to get out metal like copper. Around 4500 BCE humans figured out that they could mix tin and copper to create bronze. It was a much stronger metal used to make weapons, tools, and jewelry.

Test Type:	Paragraph #:
Description	_____
Sequence	_____
Compare and Contrast	_____
Problem and Solution	_____
Cause and Effect	_____

What's My Text Type?

ANSWERS

Paragraphs 1-3

Test Type: **Paragraph #:**
Description   ___3___
Sequence   ___2___
Compare and Contrast   ___1___
Problem and Solution   _____
Cause and Effect   _____

Paragraphs 4-6

Test Type: **Paragraph #:**
Description   _____
Sequence   ___6___
Compare and Contrast   _____
Problem and Solution   ___4___
Cause and Effect   ___5___

BATS AND THEIR AMAZING SKILLS
by Carolee Dean

INTRODUCTION

The world is full of interesting animals like bats. It's no wonder that one of the oldest Greek myths is about animals and their unusual gifts. The bat is a perfect example of how unique and special animals can be. Bats can fly, sleep upside down, and hunt in the dark. Like many other animals, they also have strong senses of hearing and smell. In comparison, people must have seemed dull and boring to the Greeks.

76-5.99

BATS ARE NOT BIRDS

Although bats can fly, they are not birds. Birds and bats are both vertebrates. They both have spines, but birds belong to the class of animals called *Aves*. Bats belong to the class of animals called *Mammalia* or mammals. Mammals have mammary glands that produce milk for nursing their young. Bats are the only

Page 1

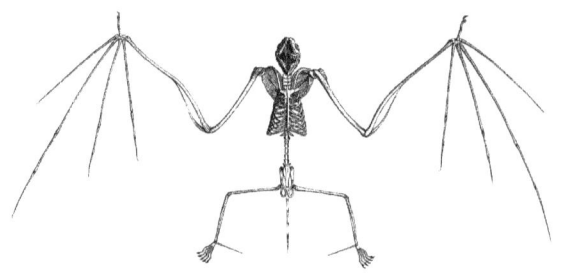

mammals that can fly. Bats belong to the order of mammals called *Chiroptera.*

If you look closely at their wings, you can see the bone structure of a hand. In fact, *Chiroptera* is a Greek word meaning "hand wing." Do you see the fingers and thumb in the skeleton image above?

105-5.83

WAYS THEY ARE DIFFERENT

Another way that bats are different from birds is that they have teeth instead of a beak. In addition, bats do not have feathers. They have very short hair on their bodies. They hunt at night and roost hanging upside down. During the day they sleep in places like trees, caves, and barns. They also like the attics of abandoned buildings. Sometimes they will even roost in homes with people living in them. Bats cannot launch into flight like birds do.

Page 2

They must fall or drop. Hanging upside down helps them to fall into flight quickly. Bats don't lay eggs. They give birth to their babies hanging upside down. When the newborn "pup" starts to fall toward the ground, the mother catches it in her wings. There aren't any birds that give birth to live babies. Only mammals do that.

140-4.33

ECHOLOCATION

Most bats have a strong sense of hearing which is helpful for hunting at night. They use a process called *echolocation*. As they fly, these bats make high-pitched sounds that humans cannot hear. The sound hits an object, makes an echo, and travels back to them. It works like an advanced radar system. Their hearing is so specialized that they can tell from the echo how far away an object is. Through *echolocation,* they not only locate the object, but they can also tell what size it is.

88-6.22

BATS CAN BE HELPFUL

You might have bats living in your attic right now, but don't worry. Bats are very helpful to humans in ways similar to birds. Some bats eat insects and help control pests that might eat your garden vegetables or flowers. Some eat nectar and help by carrying pollen from one plant to another. Other bats eat fruit and help to spread seeds. Not so helpful are vampire bats. They only drink blood. Fortunately, they prefer the blood of cows and horses. Vampire bats live in Mexico as well as Central and South America.   93-5.07

CONCLUSION

It's no wonder that in the Greek Creation Myth it seemed like the animals got all the helpful and interesting gifts. It's not true, of course. Humans have highly advanced brains, speech, and the ability to walk upright. On the other hand, they can't fly, and they don't have built-in radar systems. One thing is certain. Just like us, the ancient Greeks were fascinated by the amazing skills of animals.

70-6.55

Page 4

572 Words Total

References:

Julivert, M.S., (1994). The fascinating world of bats. Hauppauge: NY: Barron's Educational Series, Inc.

Nunez, Elissa. "Bats, Facts and Photos." *Animals*, National Geographic, https://www.nationalgeographic.com/animals/mammals/facts/bats.

Comprehension Questions about "Bats and Their Amazing Skills"

Directions: Read the article. Then RESTATE each question below on a separate piece of paper and ANSWER it in a complete sentence. Leave several blank lines between answers. You may come back later to add more information.

EXAMPLE

QUESTION: Why are bats considered mammals?

ANSWER: Bats are considered mammals because they have mammary glands and produce milk for their young.

Questions:

1. What is one skill that makes bats so unique?

2. What is one way that bats are different from birds?

3. What does *Chiroptera* mean?

4. Why do bats travel by echolocation?

5. How are bats helpful to humans?

Answers for Comprehension Questions

Make sure students have restated the question and answered it in a complete sentence.

1. What is one skill that makes bats unique?

One skill that makes bats unique is their ability to fall into flight. (Other answers may vary).

2. What is one way that bats are different from birds?

One way that bats are different from birds is that they have hair instead of feathers. (Other answers may vary).

3. What does *Chiroptera* mean?

Chiroptera means "hand wing."

4. Why do bats travel by echolocation?

Bats travel by echolocation because they hunt at night.

5. How are bats helpful to humans?

Bats are helpful to humans because they eat insects, pollinate flowers, and spread seeds.

RACE Responses

Directions: Go back to your answers for the Comprehension Questions about "Bats and Their Amazing Skills." You should have already completed **R** and **A** below. Now add **C** and **E**. **Cite** the evidence and **Explain**.

R – Restate the question

A– Answer the question

C – Cite the evidence from the text to support your answer.

E – Explain your answer

EXAMPLE

QUESTION: Why are bats considered mammals?

ANSWER (responses will vary): Bats are considered mammals because they have mammary glands and produce milk for their young. The text states, "Bats belong to a special order of mammals called *Chiroptera.*" Bats give birth to their young just like dogs and cats. Many people think that bats are birds, but they are mammals.

Comprehension Questions about the Introduction of *The Bandit*

Directions:

1. LISTEN to the Introduction section.

2. RESTATE the question on a separate piece of paper.

3. ANSWER the question in your own words in a complete sentence. Leave several blank lines between answers. You may need to come back later to add more information.

EXAMPLE

QUESTION: Why did Prometheus steal fire from Mount Olympus?

ANSWER: (answers will vary) Prometheus stole fire from Mount Olympus because he wanted a special gift for mankind.

Questions:

1. How did Prometheus hide the fire he stole from Mount Olympus?

2. What was one new thing people could do after they had the gift of fire?

3. What was the most important result of mankind having fire?

4. How did Zeus react when he realized that Prometheus had stolen fire and given it to mankind?

Answers

for Comprehension Questions

Make sure students have restated the question and answered it in a complete sentence. Answers may vary.

1. How did Prometheus hide the fire he stole from Mount Olympus?
Prometheus hid the fire he stole from Mount Olympus in a fennel stalk.

2. What was one new thing people could do after they had the gift of fire?
One of the things people could do after they had fire was to cook their food.

3. What was the most important result of mankind having fire?
The most important result of mankind having fire was that they formed groups and worked together.

4. How did Zeus react when he realized that Prometheus had stolen fire and given it to mankind?
Zeus reacted in anger when Prometheus stole fire, and he chained him to a cliff.

RACE Responses for *The Bandit*

Directions: Go back to your answers for the Comprehension Questions. You should have already completed **R** and **A** below. Now add **C** and **E**. **Cite** the evidence and **Explain**.

R – Restate the question

A– Answer the question

C – Cite the evidence from the text to support your answer.

E – Explain your answer

EXAMPLE

QUESTION: Why did Prometheus steal fire from Mount Olympus?

ANSWER: (answers will vary) Prometheus stole fire from Mount Olympus because he wanted a special gift for mankind. **The text states, "Prometheus was upset that man didn't get anything special." His brother had given away all of the gifts to the animals, and Prometheus wanted man to have a gift too.**

Graphic Organizers for Paragraph & Essay Writing

INTRODUCTION

What's Your Gift? Is a fun exploration into what attributes animals may have received when Epimetheus was passing out the "gifts." It ends with a short paragraph writing exercise.

The following graphic organizers and templates were designed to provide the building blocks needed to create paragraphs and essays. Activities build on each other starting with lists and ending with a multi-paragraph essay. Students benefit from the brainstorming stage and talking about how their information could turn into an essay even if they are not yet ready to write long responses.

1. Fun Facts – As a group, have students brainstorm things that early humans could do before they discovered fire. Then make a list of things they could only do after they had fire.

2. Balloon Brainstorm – Use the fun facts list and organize the information into the Before & After sections of the balloon. Students may draw or write responses. If time permits, show a video demonstrating how fire is used to lift hot air balloons. There is another Balloon Brainstorm available to Compare and Contrast the Greek and Maya Cultures.

3. **Venn Diagrams** are used to Compare and Contrast topics such as Prometheus versus Epimetheus and Bats versus Birds.

3. High Five Writing – Students incorporate the information from the Balloon or a Venn Diagram into one or more well-structured paragraphs.

4. I+P+P+C Compare & Contrast Essay Students follow the directions to incorporate those well-crafted paragraphs from High Five Writing into a multi-paragraph response by simply adding I (Introduction) and C (Conclusion).

What's Your Gift?
based on *No Gift for Man*
by Carolee Dean

Directions:
1. For each animal, write a sentence about which gift Epimetheus might have given them.
2. Write the name of an animal of your choice in the last box.

Animal	Gifts and Uses
dog	
cat	
rat	

2. Pick one animal and write a paragraph about that animal, its special gift, and why that gift is useful.

_____

_____

_____

_____

Fun Facts
based on *The Bandit*
by Carolee Dean

Directions:
1. Make a list of reasons why life was hard BEFORE humans discovered fire.
2. Make a list of things people could only do AFTER they discovered fire

BEFORE

AFTER

Balloon Brainstorm
based on *The Bandit*
by Carolee Dean

Directions:
1. Read *The Bandit*.
2. List or draw things that were hard for people to do without fire.
3. List or draw things people could only do with fire.

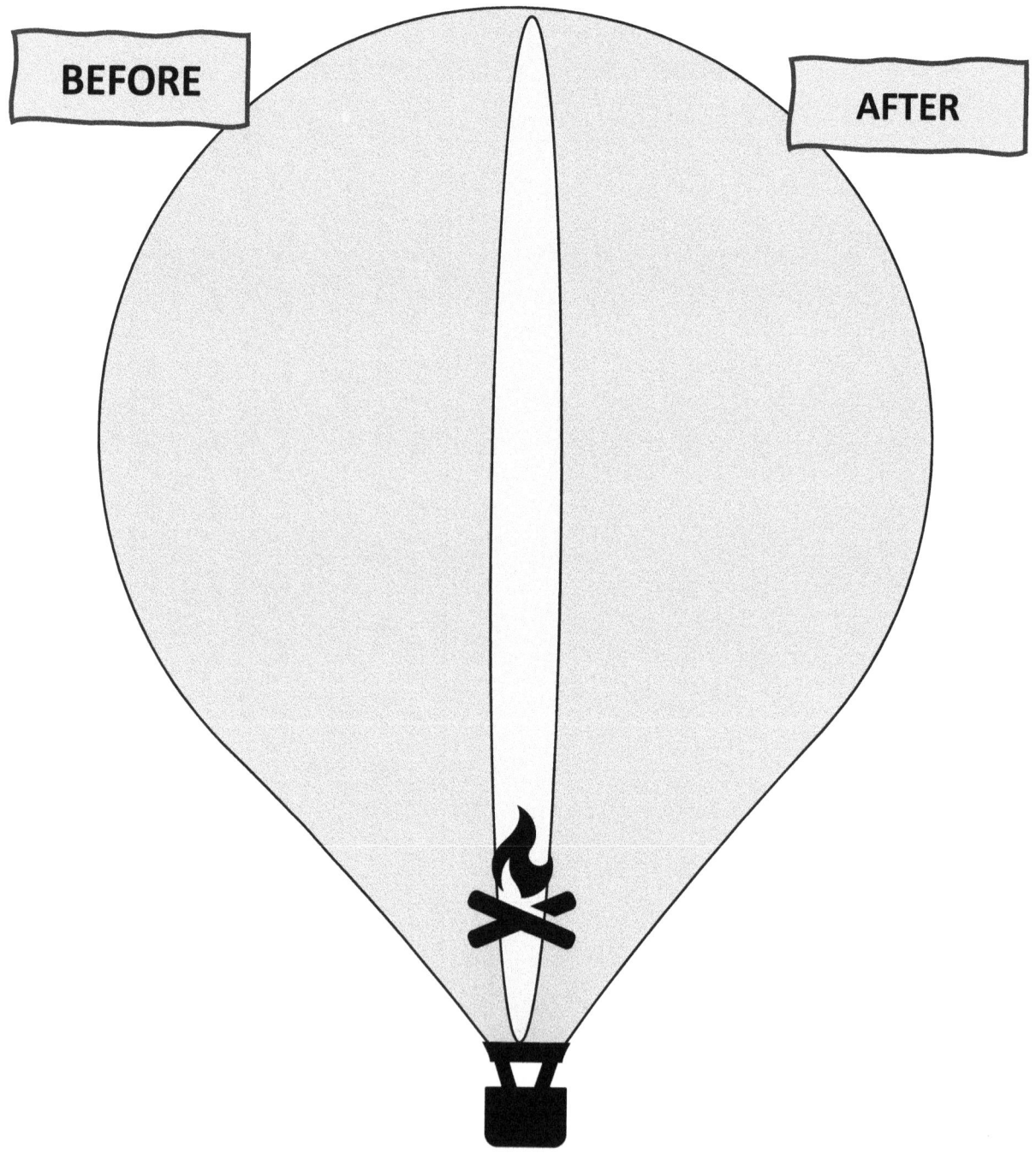

186

Balloon Brainstorm

From the Background Information Section
of *Gods and Gifts* by Carolee Dean

Directions:
1. Read or listen to the Background Information section of *Gods and Gifts*.
2. In the middle of the balloon, list the ways the Greek and Maya cultures were similar.
3. On the right and left, list the ways they were different.

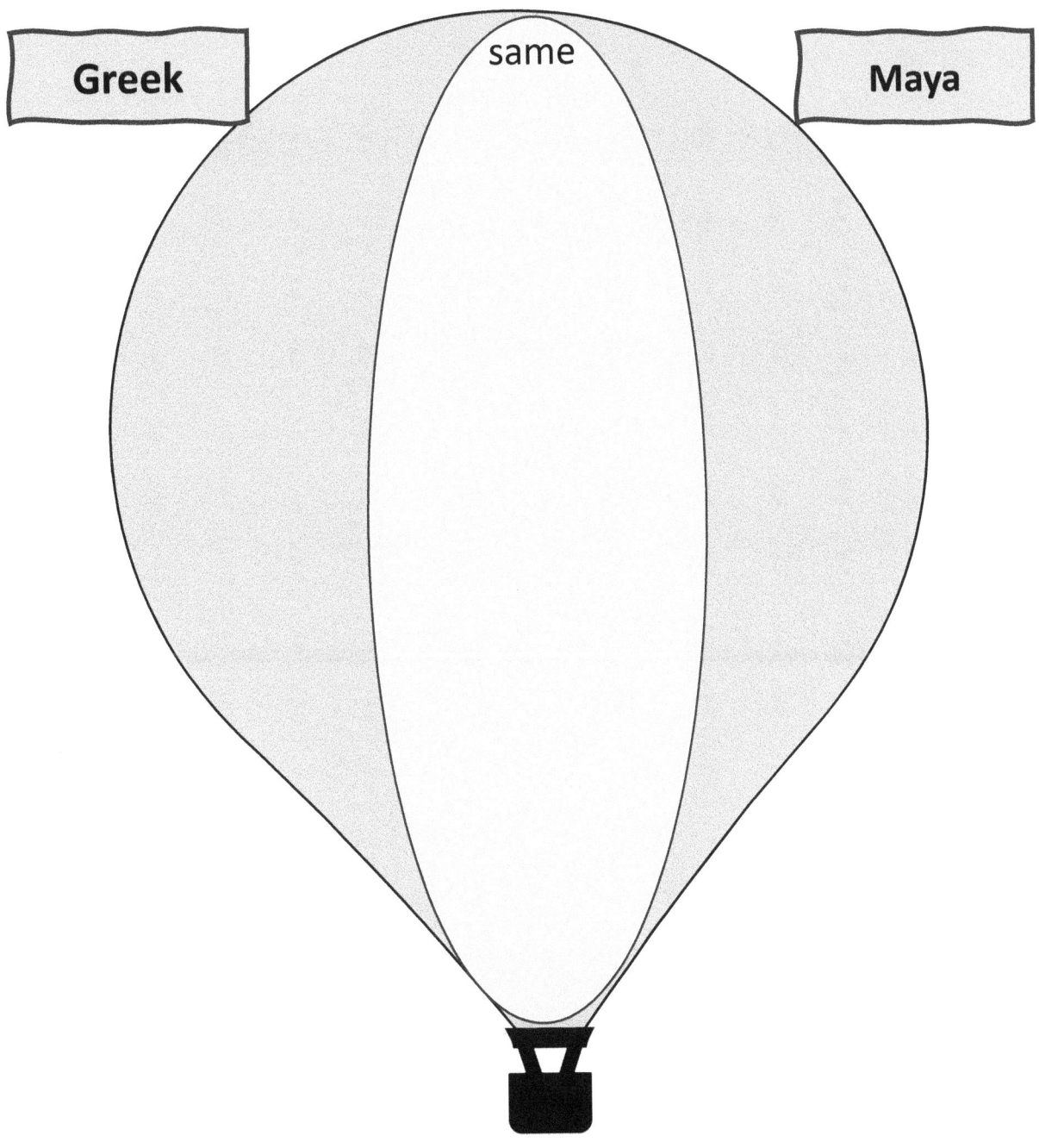

Venn Diagram
based on *No Gift for Man*
by Carolee Dean

Directions:

1. Read *No Gift for Man*.
2. List the ways that Prometheus and Epimetheus were similar.
3. List the ways that they were different.

Epimetheus   Prometheus

different

same

different

Venn Diagram

based on "Bats and Their Amazing Skills"
by Carolee Dean

Directions:
1. Read or listen to "Bats and Their Amazing Skills."
2. List the ways that bats and birds are the same.
3. List the ways that bats, and birds are different.

BATS   BIRDS

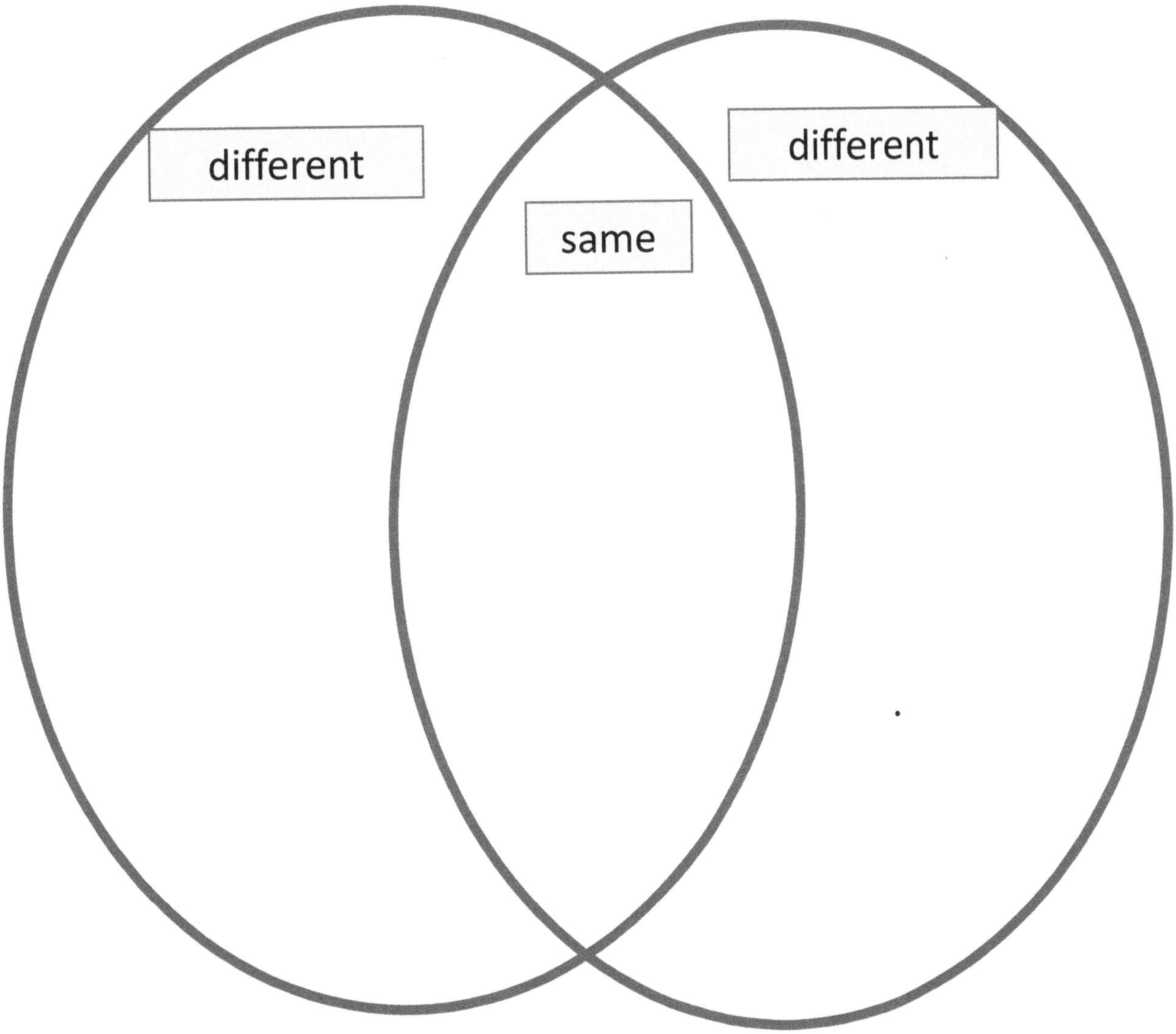

different   same   different

High Five Writing Brainstorm

Directions: Write a paragraph based on the format below.

Note: If you are writing more than one paragraph on a topic, make a separate copy of the High Five Brainstorm for each paragraph.

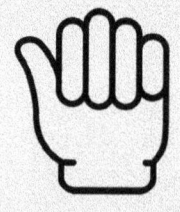

Write a 1-2 sentence INTRODUCTION:

Describe three or more supporting details in three or more separate sentences.

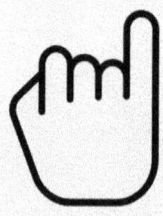

Write a conclusion.

Prompts for High Five Writing

Directions:
1. Refer to the Balloon Brainstorm or Venn Diagram for one of the topics below.
2. Choose one of the prompts for that topic and Use the High Five Writing template to create a paragraph.
3. If you plan to write more than one paragraph, use a separate High Five template for each paragraph.

Fire: Before and After
1. How was life difficult for people before they discovered fire?
2. What were some things people could do only after they discovered fire?

Greek vs. Maya
1. Describe how the Ancient Greek and Ancient Maya cultures were similar.
2. Describe how they were different.

Epimetheus vs. Prometheus
1. Describe how Epimetheus and Prometheus were similar.
2. Describe how they were different.
3. Are you more like Epimetheus or Prometheus? How? Do you plan, go with the flow, or both?

Bats vs. Birds
1. Describe how bats are similar to birds.
2. Describe how bats are different from birds.
3. Explain the skills that make bats unique.
4. Explain why the Ancient Greeks may have believed that the animals got all the good gifts.

High Five Paragraph Writing

Directions:

1. Use the *High Five Writing* template to brainstorm a paragraph.

2. Write the paragraph below.

3. Add transition words and signal words to make your paragraph flow. Signal words may be found in the Text Type Guide.

_____

_____

_____

_____

_____

_____

_____

_____

_____

_____

_____

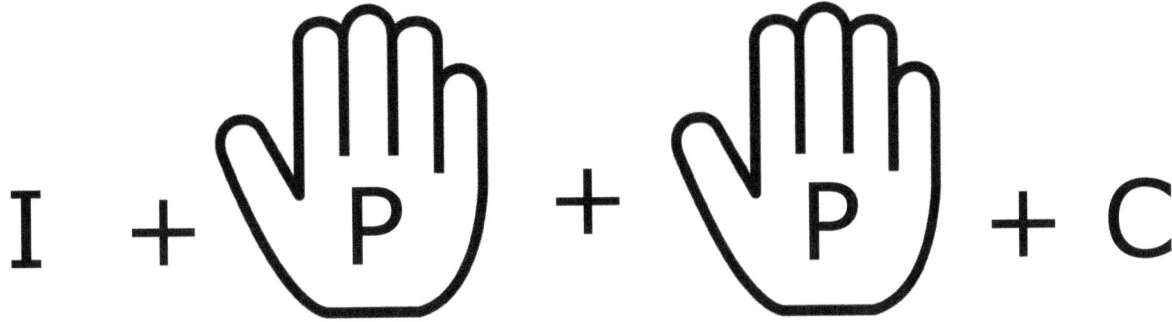

Compare & Contrast Essay
Bats and Birds

Note: It may be helpful to complete the brainstorms for paragraphs 2 and 3 before writing the introduction.

Directions:

1. **Paragraph 1** – Write an introduction explaining in a general way why some people might think bats are birds. Give hints about why this is not true, but don't give too many details.

2. **Paragraph 2** - Use a copy of the *High Five Writing* template to help you brainstorm how bats are similar to birds. Then write Paragraph 2.

3. **Paragraph 3** – Use a copy of the *High Five Writing* template to help you brainstorm how bats are different from birds. Then write Paragraph 3.

4. **Paragraph 4** – Write a conclusion stating that although bats have similarities to birds, they belong to a different animal class.

5. **EDIT** – Go back through your essay to check spelling and punctuation. Make sure there are smooth transitions between the paragraphs.

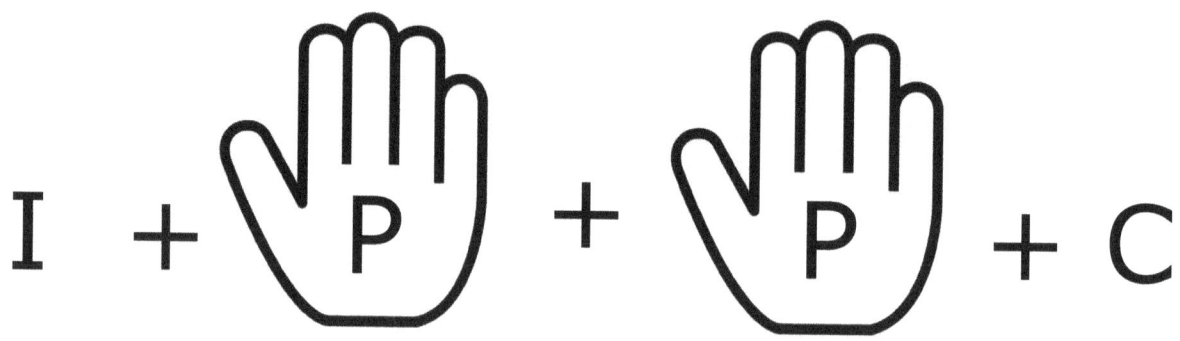

Compare & Contrast Essay
Prometheus and Epimetheus

Note: It may be helpful to complete the brainstorms for paragraphs 2 and 3 before writing the introduction.

Directions:

1. **Paragraph 1** – Write an introduction explaining in a general way how Prometheus and Epimetheus had many things in common but were still different in some important ways.

2. **Paragraph 2** - Use a copy of the *High Five Writing* template to help you brainstorm how Epimetheus and Prometheus were similar. Then write Paragraph 2.

3. **Paragraph 3** – Use a copy of the *High Five Writing* template to help you brainstorm how Epimetheus and Prometheus were different. Then write Paragraph 3.

4. **Paragraph 4** – Write a conclusion stating that although the two brothers had many similarities, their differences caused some big problems.

5. **EDIT** – Go back through your essay to check spelling and punctuation. Make sure there are smooth transitions between the paragraphs.

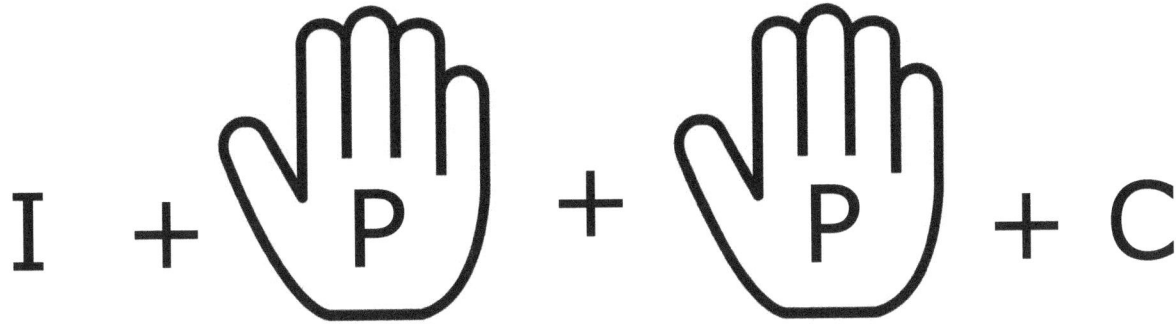

Before & After Essay
Fire

Note: It may be helpful to complete the brainstorms for paragraphs 2 and 3 before writing the introduction.

Directions:

1. **Paragraph 1** – Write an **introduction** explaining in a general way how life was very difficult for people before they had fire.

2. **Paragraph 2** - Use the paragraph that you wrote for the *High Five Writing Brainstorm* (or write one now) to discuss specifics about what life was like before mankind discovered fire. What they could do. What they couldn't do.

3. **Paragraph 3** – Use the paragraph that you wrote for the *High Five Writing Brainstorm* (or write one now) to discuss what life was like after humans discovered fire.

4. **Paragraph 4** – Write a **conclusion** discussing why fire is important for mankind.

5. **EDIT** – Go back through your essay to check spelling and punctuation. Make sure there are smooth transitions between the paragraphs.

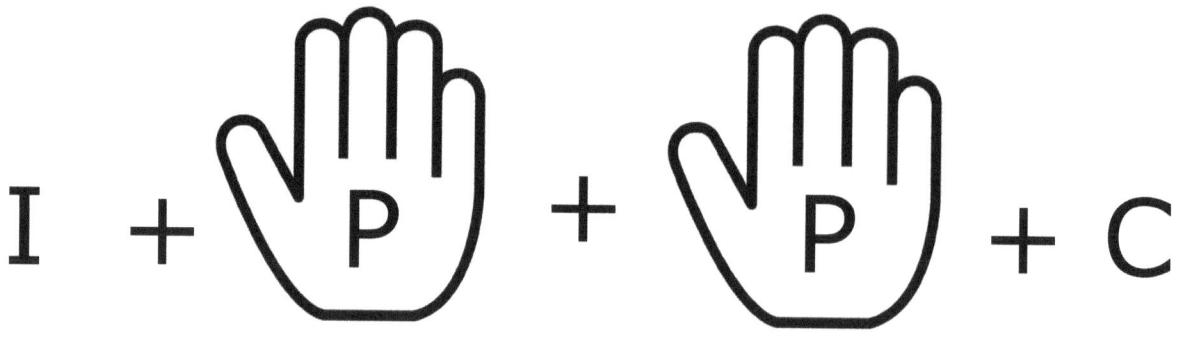

Compare & Contrast Essay
Greek and Maya

Note: It may be helpful to complete the brainstorms for paragraphs 2 and 3 before writing the introduction.

Directions:

1. **Paragraph 1** – Write an **introduction** explaining in a general way the similarities and differences of the Greek and Maya culture.

2. **Paragraph 2** - Use the paragraph that you wrote for the *High Five Writing Brainstorm* (or write one now) to discuss specific similarities between the two cultures.

3. **Paragraph 3** – Use the paragraph that you wrote for the *High Five Writing Brainstorm* (or write one now) to discuss how the two cultures were similar.

4. **Paragraph 4** – Write a **conclusion** discussing why it is important to study these two cultures.

5. **EDIT** – Go back through your essay to check spelling and punctuation. Make sure there are smooth transitions between the paragraphs.

CREATE

INTRODUCTION

CREATE is the highest level of Bloom's Revised Taxonomy because it requires a student to synthesize what has been learned and reorganize the information into something new. Within this domain, activities move from concrete to abstract and from factual to conceptual, then procedural, and finally metacognitive. A list of activities along this continuum is found below.

A. **Factual**: 1) Pick an animal from the story you have not heard of before, research it, and use the *Fun Facts* sheet to list interesting details.
2) List three ways that the discovery of fire improved everyday life for early humans. Pick one item from the list and write 2-3 sentences describing how difficult that activity was before the discovery of fire.

B. **Conceptual**: 1) Create a drawing, diorama, poem, or story about the animal you researched. Show its special gift and its habitat. 2) Look at the humorous titles on the illustration with the scrolls. Create a list of your own titles.

C. **Procedural**: Follow the steps to complete a vocabulary foldable. After studying the words, see how many you can use in a short story or paragraph.

D. **Metacognitive**: 1) Ancient cultures created myths to explain things they didn't understand like where fire came from. Imagine that you lived in an ancient culture that did not understand things like fire, storms, or disease. Make up a story about how one of these might have come to be. 2) Pretend that Pandora's Box was a lunch box. What kinds of creepy things might have come out of it?

ANIMAL FUN FACTS
based on *No Gift for Man*
by Carolee Dean

Subject: _____

Directions:
1. Pick an animal from the story you have not heard of before, research it, and list interesting details below.
2. On a separate piece of paper, use your Fun Facts to create a drawing, poem, or story about the animal you researched. Show its special gift and its habitat. You may create a diorama if you prefer.

Fun Facts

USES OF FIRE
based on *The Bandit*
by Carolee Dean

Directions:

1. List three ways that the discovery of fire improved everyday life for early humans.
2. Pick one item from the list and write 2-3 sentences describing how difficult that activity was before the discovery of fire.

Helpful Uses for Fire

Animal Gifts & Habitats
based on *No Gift for Man*
by Carolee Dean

Directions:
1. Write about the habitat for an animal you have researched below.
2. Create a drawing, diorama, poem, or story about the animal.
3. Be sure to show it using its special gift.

Habitat:

Funny Hobbies
for Zeus
based on *No Gift for Man*
by Carolee Dean

Directions:

1. Look at the humorous titles on the illustration on the next page.
2. Use your knowledge of Greek culture and mythology to create a list of your own funny titles for hobby books below.
3. Add some of your titles to the blank scrolls on the next page.
4. Add some illustrations to go with your titles.

Funny Titles

Funny Titles:
Hobbies for Zeus
based on *No Gift for Man*
by Carolee Dean

Directions: Add some of your own titles for hobby books to the blank scrolls. Then add more illustrations if you wish.

Writing with WOW Words
based on *Gods and Gifts*
by Carolee Dean

Directions:

1. Follow the steps to create a vocabulary foldable.
2. After studying the words, see how many you can use in a short story or paragraph. Write it below.

Write your story here:

Pandora's Lunch Box
Page 1
based on *The Box*
by Carolee Dean

Directions:

1. Add foods to the list that fit the sound patterns (R or S).
2. Cut out 3 disgusting foods and 1 good food. Glue them onto the lunch box on Page 3.

R Words	S Words
Disgusting Foods:	**Disgusting Foods:**
rotten rutabaga	squishy squid squares
crumbly crab cookies	spoiled spinach spaghetti
green grasshopper grits	stale toast tips
germy jerky	slimy slug smoothie
freaky frog legs	steamy snail stew
Something Good	**Something Good**
cherry Ice cream bar	sweet strawberry pie

Pandora's Lunch Box
Page 2

based on *The Box*
by Carolee Dean

Directions:

1. Make a list of bad-tasting or disgusting things that might come out of a lunch box.
2. Write down something good that is at the bottom of the lunch box.
3. Cut out 3 disgusting foods and 1 delicious food. Glue them on the lunch box on Page 3.

Disgusting Foods:

Something Good:

Pandora's Lunch Box
Page 3

based on *The Box*
by Carolee Dean

Directions:

1. Use the list you created on Page 1 or 2 to fill the lunchbox with disgusting foods.
1. At the bottom of the lunch box, put one delicious food.

Pandora opened her lunch box and out came disgusting things like:

Pandora was about to slam her lunch box shut when a little voice said, "No, don't leave me inside. I'm....

Create a Myth
based on *Gods and Gifts*
by Carolee Dean

Directions:

1. Think about what your life would be like if you lived in an ancient culture that did not understand what caused fire, storms, or disease.
2. If a child asked you to explain the cause of one of these, what might you tell them?
3. Make up a story about how fire, storms, or disease might have come to be.

Write your story here:

HOT Topics (Page 1)
Gods & Gifts by Carolee Dean
(Based on Bloom's Revised Taxonomy)
https://wordtravelpress.com/

Introduction: The following list of activities is from the decodable book, *Gods and Gifts* (Set 1, Book 4 from the HOT ROD Series). Activities have been designed to support Higher Order Thinking Skills and are arranged according to Bloom's Revised Taxonomy. This is just a sample to show the diversity of activities.

1. REMEMBER: Recall Details
A. **Factual**: Read or listen to the non-fiction article about "Bats and Their Amazing Skills." Write down as many interesting details as you can remember about bats.
B. **Conceptual**: Answer comprehension questions from "Bats and Their Amazing Skills."
C. **Procedural**: Using a blank piece of paper, draw a series of stick figures to show the action of *Gods and Gifts*. Recall and discuss what happens when humans do not receive a gift.
D. **Metacognitive**: Before reading each part of the story, have students explore what they already know about topics like Greek mythology and the origin of fire. Do this through a class discussion or a written response.

2. UNDERSTAND: Make Meaning
A. **Factual**: Copy the words and definitions from WOW Vocabulary onto index cards and study them. Use words to write sentences.
B. **Conceptual**: Study the PRO words for Morpho Mania. Then play a matching game with the definitions.
C. **Procedural**: Follow the directions to create a *Vocabulary Foldable*.
D. **Metacognitive**: Study the words on the WOW vocabulary foldable. Predict how well you will remember the words. Then Test yourself. How accurate were you in predicting your performance?

HOT Topics (Page 2)
Gods and Gifts by Carolee Dean
(Based on Bloom's Revised Taxonomy)
https://wordtravelpress.com/

3. APPLY: Use Information for a Task

A. **Factual**: Use the stick figure drawings from 1C to retell the story

B. **Conceptual**: Complete the template for *What's Your Gift?* Next to each animal's name, write what gift you think they may have received and why it is useful.

C. **Procedural**: Complete *Sentence Combining* activities for the *Sentence Construction* section. Use conjunctions to combine short sentences.

D. **Metacognitive**: Check your understanding as you read the story by asking yourself questions from the PAGES strategy. How often are you able to form a picture of what you have read? Do you use the strategy of going back to reread?

4. ANALYZE: Compare Parts to the Whole

A. **Factual**: *Complete the Sentence Construction - Identifying Complete Sentences* activity. Determine if sentences are complete or incomplete. Then decide if the sentence is missing a subject or a predicate.

B. **Conceptual**: Complete the What's My Text Type? activity and circle the signal words that help you identify the text type.

C. **Procedural**: Follow the directions in Morpho Mania for the Structured Word Inquiry matrixes and create a list of word sums. Use the word sums to complete sentences

D. **Metacognitive**: Determine which words go together in Rhyme Time #1. Circle words that rhyme and underline alliterations. Then write sentences that contain alliterations. Think about how you tackle tasks. Would rather complete all three steps for each target word before moving on OR would you prefer to do all the rhymes first, then all the alliterations, and then all the sentences? Is this how you usually work? Write a paragraph describing your process.

5. EVALUATE: Use Criteria to Make Judgements

A. **Factual**: Use the Balloon Brainstorm to list the things humans could not do before they had fire.

B. **Conceptual**: Complete a *Venn Diagram* by comparing and contrasting Epimetheus and Prometheus. Be sure to explore their strengths and weaknesses.

C. **Procedural**: Follow the High Five Writing Prompt directions to write paragraphs about Prometheus and Epimetheus.

D. **Metacognitive**: Are more like Epimetheus or Prometheus. Do you tend to make plans or jump into action? Write a short paragraph describing your organization and planning style.

6. CREATE: Reorganize Information into Something New

A. **Factual**: Create a drawing, diorama, poem, or story about an animal habitat.

B. **Conceptual**: Make a list of funny hobbies for Zeus.

C. **Procedural**: Follow the directions to create Pandora's Lunch Box.

D. **Metacognitive**: Consider what your view of the world would be like if you lived during ancient times. Write your own myth.

Read more about the **HOT ROD** (**H**igher **O**rder **T**hinking through the **R**eading **o**f **D**ecodables) **Series** at https://wordtravelpress.com/

Reference:
Anderson, L.W., & Krathwohl, D. R. (Eds.). (2001). *A taxonomy for learning, teaching, and assessing: A revision of Bloom's taxonomy of educational objectives*. New York, NY: Addison Wesley Longman, Inc.

Downloads & Online Resources

Activity Pages PDF Download

Free with the Purchase of the *Gods and Gifts Activity Book*
The download includes:
10 Game Boards for 4-in-a-Row
32 Pages of Flash Cards for Articulation and/or Reading Practice
50+ Reproducible Activity Pages
Links to Virtual Dice

To Access the Activity Pages PDF Download,
go to www.wordtravelpress.com
Visit the Page for *Gods and Gifts* (Look under Level 1 Products)
Enter the Purchaser's Code – GIFTS4U

Boom Cards

Several virtual Boom Card decks/games are available for FREE at
Boom Learning where you may set up a free account:
Target Word Flash Cards
Sound Tracker
Cognitive Flexibility Game

Other games found in the Activity Book have been turned into
Boom Cards. They may be purchased and played online for a small
additional fee.

Go to https://wow.boomlearning.com
Search for **Store>Word Travel Press.**

**If you have any issues with access, contact
info@wordtravelpress.com**

References

Anderson, L.W., & Krathwohl, D. R. (Eds.). (2001). *A taxonomy for learning, teaching, and assessing: A revision of Bloom's taxonomy of educational objectives*. New York, NY: Addison Wesley Longman, Inc.

Bowers, P. (2009). *Teaching how the written word works: Using morphological problem-solving to develop students' language skills & engagement with the written word*. Ontario, Canada: Peter Bowers

Cartwright, K.B. (2023). *Executive skills and reading comprehension: A guide for educators* (Second Edition). New York, NY: Guildford Press.

Davidson, B., & Liben, D. (2019) What a knowledge-building approach looks like in the classroom. *Perspectives on Language and Literacy*, 45 (4), 31-35

Dean, C. (2021). *Story frames for teaching literacy: Enhancing student learning through the power of storytelling*. Baltimore, MD: Paul H. Brookes Publishing Co.

Duchan, J.F. (2004). The Foundational role of schemas in children's language and literacy learning. In Stone, C.A, Sillman, E.R., Ehren B.J., & Apel, K. (Eds.), *Handbook of language and literacy*. (pp. 380-397). New York: The Guilford Press

Eggleston, R. L., Marks, R. A., Sun, X., Yu, L., Zhang, K., Nickerson, N., Hu, X., Caruso, V., & Kovelman, I. (2024). Lexical morphology as a source of risk and resilience for learning to read with dyslexia: An fNIRS investigation. *Journal of Speech, Language, and Hearing Research*. https://doi.org/2381476400030014007

Eunice Kennedy Shriver National Institute of Child Health and Human Development, NIH, DHHS. (2000). Report of the National Reading Panel: Teaching Children to Read: Reports of the Subgroups (00-4754). Washington, DC: U.S. Government Printing Office.

Farrell, L.M., & Cushen-Whte, N. (2018). Structured literacy instruction. In J.R. Birsh & S. Carreker (Eds.) *Multisensory teaching of basic language skills* (4th ed., pp. 35-72). Baltimore, MD: Paul H. Brookes Publishing Co.

Green, L. B., & Klecan-Aker, J. S. (2012). Teaching story grammar components to increase oral narrative ability: A group intervention study. *Child Language Teaching and Therapy*, 28, 263–276.

Hochman, J.C. & MacDermott-Duffy, B. (2018). Composition: Evidence-based instruction. In J.R. Birsh & S. Carreker (Eds.) *Multisensory teaching of basic language skills* (4th ed., pp. 646-676 Baltimore, MD: Paul H. Brookes Publishing Co.

Kilpatrick, D.A. (2016). Equipped for reading success: A comprehensive, step-by-step program for developing phonemic awareness and fluent word recognition. Syracuse, NY: Casey & Kirsch Publishers.

Maiden, M.E., Ampuero, M.E. & Kostewicz, D.E. (2024) A Comparison of Repeated Reading and Listening While Reading to Increase Oral Reading Fluency in Children. *Education and Treatment of Children*. **47**, 51–66. https://doi.org/10.1007/s43494-024-00121-4

Moats, L.C. (2020). Speech to print: Language Essentials for Teachers. Baltimore, MD: Paul H. Brookes Publishing Co.

Nelson, N.W. (2013). Syntax development in the school-age years: implications for assessment and intervention. *Perspectives on Language and Literacy*. 39 (3), 9-15.

Paulson, L. H. (2018). Teaching phonemic awareness. In J.R. Birsh & S. Carreker (Eds.) *Multisensory teaching of basic language skills* (4th ed., pp. 205-253). Baltimore, MD: Paul H. Brookes Publishing Co.

Ramsden, Neil. Mini Matrix Maker at www.neilramsden.co.uk/spelling/matrix

Scott, C.M., & Balthazar, C. (2013). The role of complex sentence knowledge in children with reading and writing difficulties. *Perspectives on Language and Literacy*. 39 (3), 18-26.

Shanahan, T. (2015). Are you lactating? On the importance of academic language. *Perspectives on Language and Literacy, 41*(3), 14-16.

Shanahan, T. (2019). Why children should be taught to read with more challenging texts. *Perspectives on Language and Literacy, 45*(4), 17-23.

Stein, N., & Glenn, C. (1979). An analysis of story comprehension in elementary school children. In R. Freedle (Ed.), New directions in discourse processing (Vol. 2, pp. 53-120). Norwood, NJ: Ablex.

Tunmer, W.E., & Chapman, J.W. (2012). Does set for variability mediate the influence of vocabulary knowledge on the development of word recognition skills? *Scientific Studies of Reading*, 16(2), 122-140.

Ukrainetz, T. (1998). Stickwriting stories: A quick and easy narrative representation strategy. *Language, Speech, and Hearing in Schools*, 29, 197-206.

Vadasy, P.F., Sanders, E.A., Cartwright, K.B. (2022). Cognitive flexibility in beginning decoding and encoding. *The Journal of Education for Students Placed at Risk*.

Van Cleave, W. (2014). *Writing matters: Developing sentence skills in students of all ages (Second Edition)*. Greenville, SC: W.V.C.ED.

Wright, T.S., & Neuman, S.B. (2015). The power of content-rich vocabulary instruction. *Perspectives on Language and Literacy*, 41 (3), 25-28.

Zipke, M. (2016). The importance of flexibility of pronunciation in learning to decode: A training study in set for variability. *First Language*. 36 (1), 71-86.

HOT ROD Titles

Level 1

short vowels in closed syllables and consonant blends.

suffix –s, -less, -ness, -ful

About Set 1: This set includes three colorful picture books that together form the Greek Creation Myth. They are separate books but work best as a set. Book 4 is a black-and-white version of the three stories repackaged for older students. The decodable portion is the same as in Books 1-3 but Book 4 includes numerous non-fiction connections.

Set 1, Book 1: *No Gift for Man* – Zeus asks Prometheus and his brother to fill the world with living creatures. Prometheus makes man. Epimetheus creates the animals and gives them all sorts of interesting gifts, but when man comes around for his gift, there is nothing left.

Set 1, Book 2: *The Bandit* - Prometheus steals fire from Mount Olympus to give to the humans and suffers the wrath of Zeus.

Set 1, Book 3: *The Box* –Zeus gets revenge on mankind for accepting the gift of fire. The gods create Pandora, giving her many talents and charms. Then they send her to Epimetheus as a bride and give the couple a mysterious box they are told to never open.

Book 4: *Gods and Gifts: Three Greek Myths Retold* – *No Gift for Man, The Bandit, and The Box* are told as chapters within a book for older students. It contains black-and-white illustrations. Background information about the discovery of fire, additional creation myths, and other topics are included.

Level 2

digraphs, trigraphs, combinations

(ng, ck, sh, th, ch, tch, qu, wh) single consonant n=/ng/ before /k/, and suffix –ing.

Hank the Tank: Animal in the Spotlight – A bear's life is saved through science and DNA.

Level 3

<u>long vowels in open syllables, consonant-le, suffix -ed</u>

Raven Remix – (coming Fall 2024) A fun mashup of popular titles by Edgar Allan Poe told in the format of the story poem, "The Raven."

Levels 4 & 5

<u>R-controlled and CVe Syllables</u>

Watch for more titles coming soon!

Other Resources

Check out the website to find information about Activity Books, Audio Books, and Digital Games to go with each title.

Visit www.wordtravelpress.com to find the Scope and Sequence of the series.

SIGN UP for my monthly newsletter on my website to keep up with book news, articles, and free offers.

For questions or comments, write to info@wordtravelpress.com.

Watch for additional books from the HOT ROD series. Visit www.wordtravelpress.com

Happy Reading!

Carolee Dean

Notes